# The Swimsuit Issue and Sport

*SUNY Series on Sport, Culture, and Social Relations*
*Cheryl L. Cole and Michael A. Messner, editors*

# The Swimsuit Issue and Sport

## Hegemonic Masculinity in *Sports Illustrated*

*Laurel R. Davis*

*State University of New York Press*

*Published by*
*State University of New York Press, Albany*

©*1997 State University of New York Press*

*All rights reserved*

*Printed in the United States of America*

*For information, address State University of New York Press*
*State University Plaza, Albany, NY 12246*

*Production by Dana Foote*
*Marketing by Theresa Abad Swierzowski*

**Library of Congress Cataloging-in-Publication Data**

Davis, Laurel R., 1961–
   The swimsuit issue and sport : hegemonic masculinity in Sports
illustrated / Laurel R. Davis.
      p.   cm. — (SUNY series on sport, culture, and social
relations)
   Includes bibliographical references and index.
   ISBN 0-7914-3391-9 (alk. paper). — ISBN 0-7914-3392-7 (pbk. :
alk. paper)
   1. Sports—Social aspects—United States.   2. Sports illustrated.
3. Mass media—Social aspects—United States.   4. Mass Media and
minorities—United States.   5. Developing countries in mass media—
United States   6. Sexism—United States.   7. Sexuality in popular
culture—United States.   8. Masculinity (Psychology)—United States.
9. Bathing suits—United States.   I. Title.   II. Series.
GV706.5.D39   1997
306.4'83'0973—DC20                                    96-38825
                                                         CIP

10 9 8 7 6 5 4 3 2 1

# CONTENTS

# ACKNOWLEDGMENTS

I would like to thank the following people for their assistance, support, and/or advice as I labored to study and write about the *Sports Illustrated* swimsuit issue: Cheryl Cole, Coralynn Davis, Lee Davis, Ron Davis, Margaret Carlisle Duncan, Eneida Gonzalez, Christine Grant, Bobbie Harro, Susan Joel, Paula Kilcoyne, Clay Morgan, Tina Parratt, Molly Rau, Don Sabo, Bonnie Slatton, Barbara Welch-Breder, Larry Wenner, anonymous reviewers, and the librarians at Springfield College. I thank my interview subjects for their willingness to participate in the study which serves as the basis of this book. I would especially like to thank Susan Birrell for serving as my teacher and primary advisor throughout the last decade, and Michael Messner for his support and advice on this particular project. Most of all, I thank Linda Delano for her constant intellectual, practical, and emotional support.

I gratefully acknowledge the following publishers for granting permission to quote from previously published material:

Routledge, Chapman & Hall Ltd., International Thomson Publishing Services, for excerpts from M. C. Heck, "The Ideological Dimension of Media Messages," in *Culture, Media, Language,* ed. S. Hall, D. Hobson, A. Lowe, and P. Willis (London: Hutchinson & The Centre for Contemporary Cultural Studies, 1984), pp. 122–127.

HarperCollins Publishers for material from G. Dyer, "Women and Television: An Overview," in *Boxed In: Women and Television,* ed. H. Baehr and G. Dyer (New York: Pandora, an imprint of HarperCollins Publishers Limited, 1987), p. 8.

The Speech Communication Association and Celeste M. Condit for material from C. M. Condit, "The Rhetorical Limits of Polysemy," *Critical Studies in Mass Communication* 6(2): 1989, pp. 106–7.

# Introduction

For over thirty years *Sports Illustrated* has produced an annual swimsuit issue. Each swimsuit issue features a picture of a woman model (or multiple models) in swimwear on the cover of the magazine, while a section inside the magazine contains pictures of the cover model(s) and other women models dressed in revealing swimwear. Over the years, the swimsuit issue has become a widely recognized part of United States popular culture, and an icon for many. Each year millions of people consume the swimsuit issue. Many mainstream news sources cover the annual publication of the swimsuit issue. In the last decade, magazines other than *Sports Illustrated* introduced their own swimsuit issues, and a whole new genre of magazines devoted to pictures of women in revealing swimwear emerged.

Despite the obvious popularity of the swimsuit issue, debates rage over its meaning, value, and whether it should exist at all. These debates take place within *Sports Illustrated,* within other popular media forums, and outside the media. Many appreciate the look of the models in the issue, sometimes pinning pictures from the issue on the wall. Some hide the issue from those who disapprove. Others find the swimsuit issue obscene or improper, especially for children. Some even pull the issue from library shelves. Many complain that the swimsuit spread has little to do with sports, and thus does not belong in a sports magazine. Still others critique the issue as sexist or racist. A spoof of the issue even appeared in the Doonesbury cartoon. Recently, Duncan (1993) analyzed the 1992 swimsuit issue text from an academic feminist[1] perspective. She argues that the formal structures of objectification, commodification, and voyeurism that are evident in this text disempower women and contain women's challenges to patriarchy. It is obvious that the public debate over the meaning of the swimsuit issue is fraught with emotion and that many people take action based on their interpretations of its meaning.

## Feminist Analysis with a Twist

My original interest in the swimsuit issue stemmed from my standpoint as a feminist sport sociologist. As a feminist, I was sympathetic to the view that the swimsuit issue represented the epitome of the widespread practice of sexual objectification of women in our society. Also, I objected to the fact that the swimsuit spread, which I do not define as sports coverage, was published by a magazine that is ostensibly devoted to such coverage. Although *Sports Illustrated* finds space for the swimsuit spread, the magazine has a "bad track record" when it comes to the quantity and quality of its coverage of women's athletics.

Yet, when employing a feminist perspective to analyze the swimsuit issue, I wanted to go beyond the common feminist complaint that the issue sexualizes and objectifies women. In fact, after reading a wide variety of feminist scholarship on pornography, nude bodies in art, pinups, and advertising, I became convinced that sexual images and objectification should not be seen as the enemy of feminism. Nevertheless, as opposition to the swimsuit issue seems to come mainly from feminists and from those who oppose sexual representation, it is clear that gender and sexuality are central to the meanings of the swimsuit issue in United States society. My readings of the latest feminist theory also led me to focus on issues of inequality other than sexism. Thus, although I examine the connections between the swimsuit issue and sexism in this book, I also focus on heterosexism, racism, ethnocentrism, and economic forces.

My goal is to move beyond superficial interpretations to achieve an in-depth understanding of the societal meanings of the swimsuit issue. Why is the swimsuit issue so popular with so many? Why is the issue so severely condemned by others? How is the popularity of the issue related to its condemnation, and visa versa? In order to arrive at some adequate answers to these questions, one needs to examine the interactive relationship between the production of the swimsuit issue, the swimsuit issue texts, audience interpretations of the swimsuit issue, and the wider sociopolitical and economic context.

## Studying the Mass Media

At the same time that my feminist sensibilities created an interest in initiating a formal critique of the swimsuit issue, my academic interest in the mass media was growing. As a critical scholar, my main goal is to understand and expose the ways that inequality and injustice are legitimated and maintained. This academic goal stems from my political interests. If we can understand how various forms of stratification are justified and preserved, then our scholarship can be used to devise more effective strategies to undermine these forms of stratification. Through my reading of critical theory, I became convinced that the mass media plays a central role in legitimating and maintaining various forms of stratification in contemporary Western societies.

Just as I was turning my attention to the field of critical study of the mass media, many scholars in this field were in the process of reassessing their prior theoretical positions. For many years, scholars in the field of mass communication have been engrossed in a debate over the degree to which media producers, and the texts they create, influence the perceptions and actions of audience members. In the past many scholars focused on the power of media texts to affect the audience; now they focus on the ability of the audience to interpret media texts in a wide variety of manners and their work often implies that media texts have limited or nonexistent affects on the audience.

Many scholars now view the early approaches to media analysis—the direct effects research and the uses and gratifications research—as too simplistic. Although the media help to shape categories and frameworks through which audiences perceive reality, the media do not effect perspectives or behavior in a direct and overdetermining manner. In an attempt to understand the link between production and consumption, some scholars turned to the encoding/decoding model. This model is based on the idea that producers encode meanings in texts, while audience members decode the texts to create meanings (Hall, 1984).

We now know that the meanings of media texts grow out of the interrelationships between production, the texts themselves, consumption, and the wider sociocultural environment. In other words, the meanings of any particular media text are influenced by the meanings producers intend to convey, various parts of the media production process, features of the media text itself that encourage and discourage particular interpretations, the perspectives of audience members, and elements of the wider sociocultural environment that influence the production process and the perspectives of both the producers and the audience members.

Although producers shape media texts in ways that encourage consumers to create particular interpretations of meaning in a given cultural context, these texts are not necessarily interpreted in the ways producers intend. All media texts contain the potential for multiple interpretations. Consumers, influenced by both their cultural and sub/ countercultural knowledge/beliefs, and the situation in which they consume a media text, interact with media texts to construct a variety of interpretations. Some consumers interpret texts in ways that match the intentions of producers (a preferred or dominant reading), some interpret texts in ways that deviate only slightly from the intended meaning (a negotiated reading), some understand the intended meaning but evaluate the text in ways that run counter to the producer's intent (an oppositional reading), and still others interpret the texts in ways that seem unrelated to the intentions of producers (a resistant reading) (e.g., Condit, 1989; Fiske, 1987b; Lewis, 1991; Morley, 1980).

As I read the new media theory, I noticed that there were very few attempts to examine these new ideas empirically. Very few researchers actually gather the empirical data that enables them to scrutinize the interactive relationship between production, texts, and consumption and assess the degree to which producers, texts, and audience members influence cultural meanings. The swimsuit issue seemed like an ideal media text to use for this project, as I knew that there were many different and conflicting opinions of this text.

When most researchers study the mass media, they either analyze texts, production, or consumption. Here, I not only analyze the swimsuit issue texts, but also analyze interviews with some producers of the swimsuit issue and a diverse group of audience members, and then discuss how the relationships between production, the texts, and consumption generate meaning. In addition, I attempt to describe some of the ways that the wider sociocultural environment and media texts other than the swimsuit issues influence production practices and audience interpretations. It is important to understand how meanings are created so that these meanings can be effectively affirmed, subverted, or reconstructed. The study of the swimsuit issue discussed in this book is one of the few studies that actually documents the interrelationship between media production, texts, and consumption in the empirical world.

### Getting at the Meaning of the Swimsuit Issue

My study of the swimsuit issue began with textual analysis. The texts are: the *Sports Illustrated* swimsuit issues from 1964 to 1991 and 1996 (see Appendix A), follow-up issues of *Sports Illustrated* which contain the letters of reader response to these swimsuit issues, and other media material that is related to the swimsuit issues (see Appendix B). In addition, I examined most other issues of *Sports Illustrated* from 1954 to 1991, in order to situate the swimsuit issue in the larger context of the magazine and its history.

Analysis of the swimsuit issue texts went beyond the pictures on the magazine covers and in the swimwear spreads. Other features of the swimsuit issue that I analyzed include the table of contents, magazine articles, Letter from the Publisher, titles, captions, and other written text that accompanies the pictures.

I considered a variety of intertextual forces that influence consumer interpretations of the swimsuit issue. Intertextual forces are media texts that affect consumer interpretations of the studied text. The intertextual forces that I examined include: media texts produced by *Sports Illustrated* about the swimsuit issue, media texts produced by others about the swimsuit issue, and genres that resemble the swimsuit issue. These genres include pornography, pin-ups, advertising, and nude images in art.

Not only do *Sports Illustrated* producers suggest particular interpretations of the swimsuit issue through the textual structure and content of the issue itself, but they also school the readers by encouraging particular interpretations of the issue through other media texts that they produce. These other texts include swimsuit issue videos, swimsuit issue calendars, advertisements for the calendars, advertisements for *Sports Illustrated,* and the Letters to the Editor section.

References to the swimsuit issue in the mass media by people who do not work for *Sports Illustrated* serve as evidence of the popularity of the issue and inform my understandings of audience interpretations of the issue. These references appear in many different forms, such as television, newspaper and magazine stories that define the swimsuit issue or a competitor's imitation as news, media criticism of the swimsuit issue, and actual imitations of the swimsuit issue. Some other examples of media texts that refer to the swimsuit issue include an article about dolls, a fashion column, a greeting card, and cartoons. Significant criticism of the swimsuit issue appears most often in so-called alternative publications. For example, a feminist newsletter called *Media Watch* features a feminist critique of the swimsuit issue and a report about a protest against the issue at the Time-Life Building in New York. Several magazines other than *Sports Illustrated,* such as *Sport* and *Ebony Man,* produce their own versions of the swimsuit issue. Whereas most magazines simply imitate the swimsuit issue, *Spin* magazine produced a parody of the issue (see Appendix B).

Analysis of all of the media texts mentioned above, including the swimsuit issues, involved identifying elements of the textual structure and content that appear on a regular basis and that may encourage particular interpretations of the swimsuit issues. Conventions appearing in the swimsuit spreads include the use of particular types of models, suits, body positioning, people who are pictured with the models, written content, backgrounds, props, appearance management techniques, and camera techniques. Textual analysis reveals some changes in the swimsuit issue over the years. During the textual analysis, issues related to economics, gender, sexuality, race, and nationality received special attention.

I obtained information about the production of the swimsuit issues primarily through telephone interviews with some of those who control(ed) parts of the production process and/or have a particularly informative view of this process. These producers answered questions about the production process and the meanings they attempt(ed) to express[2] (see Appendix C). My original study of the swimsuit issue featured interviews with nineteen former or current producers. This book contains information derived from only fifteen of these original interviews because four of the producers interviewed for the original study were not willing to grant me permission to use their interviews in this book. The fifteen producers include a managing editor, an advertising sales director, a director of marketing, a business manager, a circulation director, a design director, a modeling agent, a swimwear designer, two photographers, three models, and two letter department workers (see Appendix D). All but one of the interviewed producers are currently involved with the swimsuit issue or have recently been involved with the swimsuit issue. Several of the interviewed producers worked on the swimsuit issue in the 1960s and 1970s. When referring to the interviewed producers in the body of this book, I only identify the title of the producer when relevant. Other times, I simply use the term "interviewed producer."

Many, but not all, of the interviewed producers seemed guarded in their responses to my questions. Sometimes they ignored particular questions, hesitated before answering, offered a party line response, or answered questions in a superficial manner. In fact, one of these producers says that *Sports Illustrated* is "very hush-hush about any sort of information" related to the swimsuit issue. A few of these producers maintain that they need to be careful about what they say due to possible repercussions. One interviewed producer empathized with the difficulty I experienced when attempting to obtain these interviews:

> Well, people are scared to talk, because, well, even me, I was like, "Oh, my God, I don't want this to come back and haunt me."

Because if it's going to be read anywhere, it can, really. You know, it's very negative, anything that's written about you, or your name is included. If you say something to piss someone off, then it can really affect your career. So, I think a lot of people are scared.

One interviewed producer attributes the producers' hesitancy to share information about the swimsuit issue to "protests" against the issue. Obviously, many people involved with the production of the swimsuit issue feel afraid to share information about the issue in a forthright and open manner. I suspect that this hesitancy stems mainly from a fear of releasing information that can be used to buttress the case of those who oppose the issue.

The data obtained from the interviews with producers contains two different types of contradictions. Occasionally an interviewed producer contradicts herself/himself, such as stating that there is no relationship between fashion and the swimsuit issue but later in the interview explaining various ties between the fashion world and the swimsuit issue. More common than these internal contradictions are contradictions between interviewed producers. For example, some of these producers maintain that, prior to the shoots, producers preplan ideas for many of the pictures, while others maintain that producers come up with ideas for pictures more spontaneously. The data presented in this book is a composite picture of what the interviewed producers say about the swimsuit issue. Most often the contradictions appear as contradictions, as differences in opinion or approach. Other times, if sufficient evidence exists to resolve a contradiction, I present a single opinion or approach. I resolved contradictions by considering the number of producers articulating a particular point of view, the status positions that have the greatest knowledge regarding particular parts of production, and my faith in a producer's candor. I considered a producer more trustworthy if she/he did not withhold information or hesitate when answering, did not use as many routinized answers, and did not often contradict herself/himself.

In an attempt to achieve a better understanding of consumption, I conducted telephone interviews with thirty-nine consumers and thirteen librarians about the swimsuit issue. The librarians represent three junior high school, three high school, three college, and three public libraries. I selected the libraries from the telephone book of a diverse metropolitan area to represent urban, suburban, and small town communities. Questions focused on what happens to the swimsuit issue within each library (see Appendix C).

The thirty-nine consumers answered questions about their interpretations of the swimsuit issue (see Appendix C). These consumers do
not represent any general population of people on any kind of percentage basis, but they do represent a diversity of perspectives regarding
the swimsuit issue. I obtained this diversity by interviewing both women
and men, and those who appreciate, disapprove of, and hold a neutral
view of the swimsuit issue. These consumers also vary in regard to age,
race, occupation, income, sexual orientation, and degree and type of
sport participation. The degree to which the consumers read *Sports
Illustrated* and the swimsuit issue also varies (see Appendix D).

Audio tapes of the interviews with the producers, librarians, and
consumers were transcribed. Analysis involved extracting and pulling
together general information about the production and consumption of
the swimsuit issue from the interview transcripts. Analysis then consisted of considering the information about production and consumption in relationship to the information obtained from the textual analysis.

In the chapters that follow, I discuss cultural meanings of *Sports
Illustrated* and its swimsuit issue, and the various factors that help to
create these meanings. I focus on the public struggle over the meaning
of the swimsuit issue, and factors that limit and shape this struggle.

Although the swimsuit issue contains representations of women
and much of the debate about the issue focuses on the (proper) nature
of femininity, I use hegemonic masculinity as the central organizing
concept of this book. The concept of hegemonic masculinity denotes
the preeminent form that masculinity takes in the contemporary United
States. In this book, I argue that the cultural significance of the swimsuit
issue derives from the fact that it contributes to a larger project that
celebrates a politically reactionary form of contemporary masculinity.

# Sports Illustrated's Swimsuit Issue: The Rise to Popularity and Profitability

Why should anyone write or read a book about the swimsuit issue? The answer is obvious—the swimsuit issue is immensely popular in the United States, and as a result producers derive enormous profits from its publication. Any aspect of our culture that flourishes to the degree that the swimsuit issue does, despite an onslaught of criticism over the years, beckons analysis because such analysis can reveal much about the larger culture. Prior to beginning this analysis, this chapter documents the popularity and profitability of the swimsuit issue.

The other question addressed before critical analysis begins involves the origin of the swimsuit issue. Why did a sports magazine decide to publish an issue featuring pictures of women models in revealing swimwear? Surprisingly, by examining the history of the swimsuit issue I found a logical answer to this question: the swimsuit issue emerged from an earlier form of sports coverage.

## History of the Swimsuit Issue

The 1989 25th anniversary swimsuit issue documents the "official" history of the swimsuit issue (Deford, 1989). Some of the interviewed producers repeated parts of this version of history. According to both of these sources, from the birth of *Sports Illustrated* in 1954 through the early 1960s, *Sports Illustrated* included coverage of many activities that the magazine rarely covers today such as sportswear, travel, bridge, and food. Around the time that *Sports Illustrated* published the first swimsuit issue, the magazine started to place a greater emphasis on "hard sports." A few of the interviewed producers indicated that hard sports include football, basketball, and baseball rather than sports such as skiing, swimming, beach activities, golf, and tennis. The shift toward greater coverage of hard sports coincided with the economic success of the magazine; only after the mid-1960s did *Sports Illustrated* make a profit.

According to the official version of history (Deford, 1989), on January 21, 1963, *Sports Illustrated* ran a story about travel in the tropics. The cover of this magazine pictured a young woman swimming in the water near Puerto Vallarta, Mexico. The managing editor decided to run this story and picture to fill what *Sports Illustrated* producers perceived as a void in sports news between football bowl games and baseball spring training.[1] The following January, the managing editor ran what he calls "the original" swimsuit issue, which featured a "bathing beauty" (Deford, 1989, p. 41) on the cover and five pages of pictures of women models in swimsuits.

As the story goes, in the early years the managing editor brought in the long-standing senior editor to work on the swimsuit issue and to make it more sexy. This senior editor began by making the decision to photograph young women with a "California"/"healthy look" (Deford, 1989, p. 41) instead of high fashion models. Deford (1989), author of this official historical account, suggests that the sexual connotations of the swimsuit issue spawned controversy about the issue since its beginning.

According to some of the interviewed producers, the early swimsuit issues placed a bit more emphasis on tourism and fashion, and blended into the typical weekly coverage of the magazine. As one interviewed producer puts it, nowadays the swimsuit issue seems to have "a little less relation to things [in] the rest of the magazine." Some interviewed producers note that over the years the swimsuit issue became much more central to *Sports Illustrated* magazine, and its publication became a major public event. As one of these producers comments:

> When they started out to do it, many years ago, it was very modest and a kind of curious diversion. It became a *phenomenon!* It became so successful that it has a life of its own, so to speak . . . It was a different time [back then] . . . [and] it kind of disappeared into the magazine as a frivolous extra thing we did.

Now it has such a major presence . . . because it's something in and of itself.

Comparative textual analysis of the pre-1964 and post-1964 issues of *Sports Illustrated* reveals even more about the history of the swimsuit issue. Prior to 1964, *Sports Illustrated* contained coverage that set a precedent for the swimsuit issues that followed.

In the early years of *Sports Illustrated,* articles and advertisements about travel more commonly appeared in the magazine than in recent years. This travel coverage most often focused on adventures in (post)colonialized countries[2], and sport vacations and beach activities in the southern United States and (post)colonialized countries. The older issues of *Sports Illustrated* contained more coverage of water sports, such as skin diving and surfing, probably because they featured more coverage of travel. Although recent issues of the magazine feature the theme of travel in (post)colonialized lands less often than the issues from the past, this theme still appears in some of its articles and advertisements.

Early travel articles and advertisements in *Sports Illustrated* represented people from (post)colonialized countries in the same ways that these people appear in the swimsuit issue. In both cases, people from these countries commonly serve or assist white Westerners by serving food and drink, performing physical labor, and entertaining in ways that many Western people perceive as "exotic." Both the pre-1964 texts and the swimsuit issues suggest that (post)colonialized countries are "untouched" or undiscovered, and populated with exotic and endangered wildlife and with people who are exotic, primitive, natural, friendly, and polite.

The early issues of *Sports Illustrated* also contained a greater emphasis on fashion than do current issues. These early issues covered both women's and men's fashion on a regular basis, and even included a regular feature called "The Sporting Look." In the late 1950s and early 1960s the magazine sponsored a "Sportswear Design Award." In the "Memo From the Publisher" on November 22, 1954, the publisher discussed why *Sports Illustrated* covers fashion, stating that " . . . it is a vital part of the story and history of sport itself, telling each week in pictures and a few words what sports do for clothes and what clothes do for sports" (p. 1). In the early fashion spreads, the pictured clothing included items worn for both spectating and participating in sport, as well as items inappropriate for sport activities but influenced by sport fashion. This coverage focused mainly on women's clothing, and tended to display the clothing on slim white models. *Sports Illustrated* covered fashion quite extensively up until the mid-1970s, although the issues from the mid-1960s seem to carry the most comprehensive coverage. After the mid-1970s, the amount of fashion coverage slowly declined, and by the mid-1980s fashion coverage appeared only on an occasional basis.

In addition to articles about fashion, *Sports Illustrated* magazine has always contained advertisements for clothing. In the early years, these advertisements promoted both men's and women's clothing, but within a few years advertisements for men's clothing began to predominate. Since the mid-1960s, almost all of the advertised clothes are for men. Advertisements for men's and women's swimsuits appeared regularly until the early 1960s. For most of the 1960s, advertisements for men's swimsuits predominated. Since the late 1960s, advertisements for men's and women's swimwear appear only occasionally. All of this early attention to fashion, in both articles and advertisements, laid the foundation for the swimsuit issue.

It is interesting that the producers of *Sports Illustrated* name 1964 as the year the magazine published its first swimsuit issue given that prior to 1964 *Sports Illustrated* featured many swimsuit and beachwear spreads,[3] and even a few covers that pictured a woman in swimwear.[4] For example, the cover of a 1954 *Sports Illustrated* issue pictured a woman in a bathing suit in the surf (August 30). Inside this issue, an article about surfbathing featured another picture of a woman in a swimsuit along with a comment about the woman's attractiveness. Two other issues in 1954 contained fashion spreads that highlighted women's swimwear. In 1955, *Sports Illustrated* included an article about the West Coast swimwear industry (November 28). An advertisement for the magazine published in the same year states, among other things, that *Sports Illustrated* "sets the pace" in swimwear styles (June 20, p. 69).

Many of the conventions of posing featured in this early coverage of swimwear resemble those in the "official" swimsuit issues, including those that commonly connote subordination and/or sexuality. These conventions include a leg and head cant (meaning that the model bends one knee slightly over the other leg and tilts her head), a twisted body, and an autoerotic look, all of which I discuss later in this book. As in the official swimsuit issues, the early coverage included revealing swimwear and ways of wearing the swimwear that suggest sexual meaning. For example, one picture in 1960 displayed the crack between a woman's buttocks, while another picture in the same issue featured a woman with the top of her suit untied (August 22).

The pre-1964 coverage, like the coverage in the swimsuit issues, commonly named the swimwear prices, the swimsuit designers/manufacturers, and the locations featured in the picture backgrounds. Also like the swimsuit issues, some of the early coverage contained information about the location of the shoot. Yet, in the early years this information included more details about how to travel and where to stay, and sometimes provided telephone numbers and/or addresses which could be used to obtain more information.

The features of the pre-1964 coverage that most closely resemble the features of swimsuit issues are the topics in the written texts that accompany the pictures. These written texts focus on the lives of the models, beauty of the models, swimwear styles, and warm places to travel for vacation. Even in the early years, the written texts suggested that the pictures, suits, and/or models connoted sensual or sexual meaning. The pre-1964 coverage commonly included discussion about revealing clothing.[5] For example, in the December 24, 1962 issue, a passage about women's swimwear said that a particular fashion designer ". . . has vastly increased the amount of themselves that women care to bare at the beach" (p. 71).

Also similar to the swimsuit issues, in the early years *Sports Illustrated* published some reader responses to the swimsuit coverage in the Letters to the Editor section, although compared to later years the editors printed these letters on a less regular basis and in smaller numbers. The themes that showed up in these early letters also appear in the later letters about the swimsuit issues. These themes include appreciation of the beauty and sexuality of the models by men readers (January 3, 1955; July 25, 1958) and complaints that the magazine should stick to covering sports (June 5, 1961).

Like the swimsuit issues, some of the written texts in early swimwear spreads encouraged readers to view the spreads as aesthetic and sexual display for men. For example, the text of a women's swimwear spread published in 1954 said, "The American male can take a look at the shape of the future on these four pages . . ." (December 20, p. 45). In this same issue, in a printed letter to the editor, a man stated that he sent *Sports Illustrated* some guidelines on "girl watching," "to help you and your readers get more pleasure out of this wonderful pastime [because] I can see by your November 29th issue that my hobby (girl watching) has now been officially recognized as a sport" (p. 68). The editors not only reinforced this interpretation of the swimsuit spread by printing this letter, but they also printed some of the guidelines with cartoon illustrations and a small picture of a woman in a bikini labeled as "girl." The editor commented: "See cuts for elementary rules and a few species to be found in this fascinating sport. For a

field report on the startling new variety, the compressed poolpet, see
p. 45" (p. 68).

One of the major differences between the pre-1964 swimwear
coverage and the official swimsuit issues is that the pre-1964 coverage
featured men's and occasionally children's swimwear, although women's
swimwear predominated. After 1962, the magazine rarely displays men's
swimsuit fashion and men's swimwear never appears in the swimsuit
issue itself, with a couple of negligible exceptions in 1966 and 1970.

Another difference between the early and later swimwear coverage is that the early coverage placed a stronger emphasis on the
fashions themselves. In fact, the early coverage often featured extensive
discussion of fashion information, such as materials and styles.[6] In
comparison to the swimsuit issues, the early coverage seemed to place
a greater emphasis on the display of clothing for women and less
emphasis on the display of models' bodies for men. Even as late as
1965, an article about women's swimwear read, " . . . you can be as
bare as your body is beautiful" (January 28, p. 36), indicating that the
text was addressing women readers.

Another indication that the early coverage placed a greater emphasis on fashion is that until the mid-1970s *Sports Illustrated* regularly
published the names of stores where the reader could purchase the
swimwear. Also, the celebrity status of the models seemed less significant in the early years. In fact, in some of the early coverage the
producers used people who were not models to display the swimwear,
and this coverage included spreads that neglected to report the models'
names.

After 1964, *Sports Illustrated* continued to cover swimwear in
issues other than those deemed official swimsuit issues. For example,
*Sports Illustrated* covered both men's and women's beachwear on May
18, 1964 and May 24, 1965, men's swimwear on April 20, 1970, and
women's competitive swimwear on July 29, 1968 and August 12, 1974.
On July 17, 1967 and August 20, 1973 the magazine featured swimwear
along with other articles of clothing.

My analysis reveals that 1964 is the approximate time when the
swimwear coverage in *Sport Illustrated* changed directions. Nineteen
sixty-three marks the beginning of an annual January/February publication date. Nineteen sixty-four marks the approximate time when
*Sports Illustrated* began to print letters of reader response to the swimsuit coverage on a regular basis; the long-standing senior editor assumed a leadership role over the production of the issue; and the
coverage of swimwear shifted from a focus on both men's and women's

swimwear to a focus only on women's swimwear. Perhaps most importantly, 1964 marks the approximate time when the swimwear coverage began to encourage the view that the ideal consumers are men rather than women and men, which would suggest a shift in purpose, away from a primary focus on the display of fashion toward a primary focus on the display of women's bodies.

By the late 1970s, the published letters to the editor reveal that many consumers viewed *Sports Illustrated's* swimsuit issue as a popular United States icon. By the mid-1970s, it is clear some consumers in one major metropolitan area defined the swimsuit issue as pin-up material, because these consumers ripped out many of the pages of the swimsuit issues in library copies published after this date. By 1980 consumers ripped out practically all of the pages in these library copies, confirming the issue's pin-up status.

In conclusion, the emergence of the swimsuit issue in *Sports Illustrated* in 1964 is no surprise if one considers the early coverage in *Sports Illustrated*, the probable motives of the producers, and general changes in the magazine over the years. Prior to 1964, the magazine producers utilized a broad definition of sport that included travel and fashion. The early coverage suggested that readers were women as well as men, and contained a heavy emphasis on fashion as well as the display of women's bodies.

During the 1960s, *Sports Illustrated* began to employ a more narrow definition of sport which focused on elite men's spectator sports. The pursuit of profit probably prompted this shift, because these sports receive extensive coverage on television and thus attract a large number of dedicated consumers. With this shift in coverage in the mid-1960s, *Sports Illustrated* finally became a profitable venture. Coverage of fashion and travel, and coverage (that seems) aimed at wealthy sport participants, declined. Eventually, practically the only time that the magazine devoted any attention to fashion and travel occurred when the magazine published its yearly swimsuit issue. Over the years, the swimsuit issue significantly increased in size and became less related to the magazine's general content. Consumers increasingly defined the issue as expressing sexual meaning for male consumers and as a central part of *Sports Illustrated*.

## Popularity of the Swimsuit Issue

The producers of *Sports Illustrated* possess much information that illustrates the popularity of the swimsuit issue. In fact, some producers contend that *Sports Illustrated* publishes the swimsuit issue because of public demand. As one interviewed producer claims, *Sports Illustrated* publishes the issue "because it's looked forward to each year." Of course, *Sports Illustrated* itself plays a part in creating this "demand."

The fame and prestige of those involved in the production of the swimsuit issue provide evidence of the issue's popularity. The interviewed producers observe that working on the swimsuit issue enhances the prestige of the models, swimwear companies, and photographers. For example, one interviewed model says that the issue is "powerful" because, "it's almost like it makes me legitimate, or it makes me famous, . . . [a] celebrity rather than just a model." An interviewed photographer comments, "To work on the swimsuit issue is the premiere magazine assignment of the year in the United States . . . It's a real honor to do it."

The interviewed producers cite public reactions to the swimsuit issue as proof of its popularity. For example, one interviewed producer states, "It's something everyone knows comes around once a year . . . Everyone checks it out . . . It's like required reading or viewing." An interviewed worker from the Letters Department at *Sports Illustrated* reports that the swimsuit issue results in twice as much mail as other issues of the magazine. An interviewed model states that after posing for the swimsuit issue, "I got lots of fan mail, and I didn't normally get fan mail . . . I would get sent my [picture from the swimsuit issue] and people asking me to autograph it and send it back . . . [for their] collection."

The interviewed producers note that attention of the mass media to the swimsuit issue also demonstrates its popularity. One talked about television coverage of the swimsuit issue. Another producer simply asserts, "There's a lot of publicity involved with it now."

Advertisers take advantage of the popularity of the swimsuit issue to promote their products. They use the swimsuit issue theme in two ways: hiring swimsuit issue models as spokespeople for their products, and featuring a swimsuit issue theme in advertisements for their products in the swimsuit issue. The especially large audience drawn to the swimsuit issue motivates a few companies to advertise their products only in the swimsuit issue, not in other issues of *Sports Illustrated.*

Most consumers view the swimsuit issue as a prominent part of United States culture. For example, in 1979 one man writes about the swimsuit issue as "an American tradition" (February 19, p. 76), along with baseball, hot dogs, and Mom. An interviewed consumer calls the purchase of the issue by men "a cult-type thing." Like the producers, many consumers observe that the publication of the swimsuit issue each year is treated as news. As one interviewed consumer exclaims:

> Name another magazine that comes out with one specific issue in the entire year, and literally have that issue reported in all the other media. You hear it on TV, "Ooh! The *Sports Illustrated* swimsuit issue is out, and it's selling like hot cakes!"

Even those interviewed consumers who do not read the issue on a regular basis mention that their curiosity is aroused due to all the "hype" and "attention it gets," which often moves them to look at the issue. Consumers observe that the issue is a significant topic in public discourse. As one interviewed consumer remarks, "Everyone talks about it."

On average, "regular" issues of *Sports Illustrated* sell 3.3 million copies; in contrast the swimsuit issue sells about 5 million copies. Although ninety-five to ninety-seven percent of the readers of the general issues of *Sports Illustrated* subscribe to the magazine, only sixty-six percent of the swimsuit issue readers subscribe. As an interviewed producer explains, "Instead of selling 150 or 200,000 copies [of regular issues of *Sports Illustrated*] on newsstands, [the swimsuit] issue sells a couple million copies on newsstands." More specifically, the Audit Bureau of Circulation (1991) reports that average newsstand circulation for *Sports Illustrated* magazine for a six month period in 1991 was 149,540, whereas the 1991 swimsuit issue sold 1,453,547 copies on the newsstand. So, in 1991 the swimsuit issue sold approximately ten times more copies on the newsstand than did other issues of *Sports Illustrated*. Obviously, this kind of popularity is going to result in enormous profit.

## Profitability of the Swimsuit Issue

*Sports Illustrated* charges more for advertisements in the swimsuit issue than for advertisements in regular issues of the magazine. Data obtained from *Sports Illustrated* reveal that in 1994 rates for full page four-color advertisements in the national edition cost about eight percent more for the swimsuit issue than for other issues of the magazine. *Sports Illustrated* also offers an option of advertising in only half of the national edition, and the rates for full page four-color advertisements in this case cost about seventeen percent more for the swimsuit issue than for other issues of the magazine (Time, Inc., 1993a; 1993b). In 1989, companies paid approximately twenty-eight percent more to advertise in the swimsuit issue than in other issues of *Sports Illustrated* (Leiberman, 1989).

The interviewed producers report that profits from the swimsuit issue and its spin-off products are significant, but they would not give specific figures. An interviewed business manager states that the swimsuit issue is "very profitable" and the calendar and diary "does well." In 1989, the year that *Sports Illustrated* published its twenty-fifth anniversary swimsuit issue, experts projected that *Sports Illustrated* would make approximately thirty million dollars from the issue through advertising, circulation, and spin-off revenue (e.g., Adler, Darnton & Barrett, 1989; DeMont, 1989; Elliott, 1989; Lieberman, 1989). Some predicted that advertising would account for approximately half of these revenues. Experts forecasted that swimsuit issue videos and calendars would bring in hundreds of thousands of dollars in 1989 (Lieberman, 1989). One interviewed producer believes that the 1989 swimsuit issue video sold more copies than any (other) sports video. The publisher of *Sports Illustrated* reports that advertising revenues for the 1993 swimsuit issue were about twelve million dollars (Elliott, 1994). Obviously, with this kind of profit at stake, producers are not likely to cater to those who demand that *Sports Illustrated* cease to publish the swimsuit issue.

What is it about the swimsuit issue that generates this much popularity and profit? To answer this question, one needs to find out what consumers define as the content of the swimsuit issue, and then figure out why this content is appealing to so many consumers.

# The Basic Content: "Ideally Beautiful and Sexy Women for Men"

Interestingly, consumers, for the most part, agree with each other in regard to the basic content of the swimsuit issues and the type of people who are most likely to consume these issues. Some elements of the swimsuit issue texts, production, consumption, and the sociocultural environment help to create this agreement.

### The Basic Content: Ideal Women's Bodies

Consumers clearly feel that producers design the swimsuit issue to display women's bodies. As one interviewed consumer expresses it, the swimsuit issue is about "women showing off their bodies." Consumers believe that the swimsuit issue does not just focus on *any* women or *any* bodies, but on feminine women and their ideally beautiful and sexy bodies.

That consumers declare beauty to be an essential component of the swimsuit issue is illustrated by one interviewed consumer's statement that the issue consists of "beautiful girls in swimwear." Most consumers assume mainstream or dominant definitions of beauty, and they rarely articulate critiques of these socially created beauty standards. Only two of the interviewed consumers, both people of color, critique these standards in any way.

Most consumers also name sexuality as a central element of the swimsuit issue content. One interviewed consumer calls the swimsuit issue "cheesecake," while another describes it as "soft-core pornography." Most of the interviewed consumers immediately and forthrightly articulated this meaning, yet other interviewed consumers waited until part way into the interview to suggest this meaning and seemed nervous in stating it. Societal taboos regarding open conversations about sexuality likely contributed to the hesitancy on the part of these consumers to freely discuss sexual meaning, especially with an unknown person.

Finally, consumers view the swimsuit issue models as symbols of femininity, womanhood, or womens' difference from men. For example, in the February 22, 1982 issue of *Sports Illustrated*, a letter writer states that the swimsuit issue is a relief from the winter outfits he currently sees, which he complains do not help to distinguish between men and women: "Do you realize it's 20° below zero here in Colorado . . . and we can't even tell women from men because of the multilayers of clothing we're wearing . . . I love [the swimsuit issue]" (p. 72). A 1984 letter writer declares that, "In an age of transvestite rock stars, bisexuality and drug abuse in sport, I find it wholesome to see that boys can still be boys, and girls can still be girls" (March 12, p. 86). Later I will discuss the role that perceived physical gender difference plays in legitimating the current gender order.

### The Ideal Readers: Men

Consumers consensus goes beyond the basic content of the swimsuit issue, as they also concur about who reads the swimsuit issue. Most consumers maintain that men and boys constitute the primary consumers of the swimsuit issue, and that women either do not consume the issue much at all or represent less significant consumers. For example, the interviewed consumers describe the swimsuit issue as "geared towards men," "a draw for men," and "male-oriented." By the 1970s consumers whose letters appear in the Letters to the Editor section of *Sports Illustrated* began to explicitly define the swimsuit issue as a form of representation for men. For example, one writer describes the swimsuit issue as something " . . . that sons hide under mattresses" (February 19, 1979, p. 78), while another claims that the issue features pictures of "girlie stuff to leave our sports-loving men with their tongues hanging out" (February 22, 1982, p. 72).

### Denotative versus Connotative Level Meaning

Awareness of antagonistic opinions of the swimsuit issue, and the recently-produced academic literature that claims that audience members create divergent interpretations of all media texts, led me to anticipate that there would be little agreement among consumers regarding the meaning of the swimsuit issue. Thus, I was surprised to find consensus among consumers regarding the basic content and ideal readers of the issue. At first I was at a loss to explain this finding, but reading an article by Celeste Michelle Condit (1989) proved illuminating.

Condit (1989) maintains that it is useful to distinguish between denotative and connotative level meanings. The distinction between these two levels of meaning is purely analytical (Hall, 1984; Heck, 1984). Denotation "simply refers to the first system of signification which generates a second system 'wider than the first' (which is the plane of connotation)" (Heck, 1984, p. 125). As Heck (1984) explains:

> In this sense "denotation" is nothing more than a useful rule for distinguishing, in any particular instance or operation, those connotations which have become naturalized and those which, not being so fixed, provide the opportunity for more extensive ideological representations. (p. 126)

Thus, denotative meanings are those "that are defined by the code most widely in use" (Heck, 1984, p. 124), those that have "been fixed in conventional usage and [are] widely and apparently 'naturally' employed within a language community" (Heck, 1984, p. 126). As Hall (1984) observes, at the level of denotation, encodings and decodings often have an "achieved equivalence" (p. 132).

Most struggle over meaning takes place at the connotative level (Hall, 1984). Condit (1989) argues that it is probably common for an audience to create similar interpretations of denotative level meaning, or the basic content of a media text, but then to evaluate this text in different ways, thus producing different connotative level interpretations:

> Polyvalence occurs when the audience members share understandings of the denotations of a text but disagree about the valuation of these denotations to such a degree that they produce notably different interpretations . . . Different respondents may similarly understand the messages that a text seeks to convey. They may, however, see the text as rhetorical—as urging positions upon them—and make their own selections among and evaluations of those pervasive messages. (pp. 106–107)

Here, Condit (1989) is talking about oppositional readings. Justin Lewis (1991) contends that some audience members do challenge denotative level meanings, thus producing resistant readings.

My findings regarding consumer interpretations of the swimsuit issue reaffirm the findings of Condit (1989), that, within a given culture, different interpretations of meaning occur primarily at the connotative level. Within a common culture, the different sub/countercultural discourses understood by various categories of consumers mainly influence how they evaluate the basic content of a media text, not what they define as this content. Certainly, consumers create resistant readings of many media texts, where the reading does not rest upon the same denotative level meanings as dominant, negotiated, and oppositional readings. Yet, I did not discover any such resistant readings of the swimsuit issue.

### Factors That Encourage Denotative Level Consensus

Many factors help to produce relative consensus among consumers regarding the basic content and ideal readers of the swimsuit issue. Although I do not have room in this book to document all of these factors and the relationships between them, here I provide some examples of how these factors contribute to the consensus.

### The Ideas of Producers

Most of the interviewed producers indicate that they design the swimsuit issue to highlight the models' bodies. Some of the interviewed producers point out that the backgrounds and the swimwear are secondary to the models' bodies. For example, an interviewed model argues:

> Usually if you're in a fashion shoot, what people are interested in is having the clothes look good. In this case, it's really making sure that your body looks good . . . I don't think there's anyway of getting around the fact that what you're really showing is not bathing suits, it's bodies . . . It's about bodies.

Some of the interviewed producers imply that they design the swimsuit issue to express femininity and/or ideal beauty. An interviewed photographer says he hopes that the reader will "see that he's got a really beautiful woman in front of him." An interviewed model states that the producers try to capture "the essence of woman."

One interviewed photographer notes that when he works on the swimsuit issue he tries to convey "a lot of sensuality as well as sexuality." Although almost all of the interviewed producers named sexual meaning as central to the swimsuit issue, some neglected to name or discuss this meaning. I asked these producers why many consumers interpret the issue as expressing sexual meaning. They responded in two ways, arguing that the standpoint of the consumers prompts this interpretation, and asserting that "There's a component of erotic appeal in almost every way that people appreciate other people for their physical skills." Since much of the controversy surrounding the swimsuit issue is related to sexual meaning, it is not surprising that some of the producers deny that they intentionally produce this meaning.

When asked about the audience they address when they create the swimsuit issue, some of the interviewed producers claim that they do not shape the issue with any specific types of readers in mind. A few remark that they consider their colleagues from the media industry, while others say that they keep the demographic data of *Sports Illustrated* in mind. Most of the interviewed producers imply or directly state that they fashion the issue primarily for men and boys. For example, one interviewed producer declares that the issue is "clearly for a male audience."

*The Production Process*

A variety of production practices help to create the consensus among consumers regarding the denotative level meaning of the swimsuit issue. These practices include: the small number of influential producers, the communication practices used by producers, body management and posing techniques, picture modifications, and the criteria employed during selection of pictorial background, photographers, models, swimwear, and the pictures themselves.

The small number of influential producers, and the power these producers have to select other producers that agree to shape the issue in the desired manner, enable them to create texts that convey little ambiguity. Only a few producers make decisions that directly and substantially impact on the meanings encoded into the text. The senior editor and managing editor have the most significant impact, while the design director and photographer(s) also exert a considerable influence. Other producers contribute to the encoded meanings in a much less consequential way. The managing editor occupies the position with the most power over the content of *Sports Illustrated,* and possesses final authority over the content of the swimsuit issue. As the interviewed managing editor notes, "I contribute a lot in that I express my desire and my concern for a certain kind of story, and it's the responsibility of the senior editor . . . to deliver that for me." The senior editor and the assistant(s) to the senior editor hold the only jobs at *Sports Illustrated* that solely involve duties related to the swimsuit issue. The senior editor manages the daily work on the swimsuit issue and makes most of the decisions related to the issue. For example, the senior editor selects the swimwear, hires the models, directs the shoot, helps to choose the pictures, and creates the written text for the spread.

The communication that takes place between the producers increases the degree of agreement among these producers regarding the meanings they attempt to express during the encoding phase. Producers insist that those who work on the swimsuit issue possess the ability to work well together. In the 1990 swimsuit issue calendar, the senior editor writes that there must be chemistry, "Between the model and me, the photographer, the rest of the crew and, most of all, the reader." Producers require that those who work on the swimsuit issue commit themselves to the mission of the issue, which seems to mean that they must submit to those who most understand this mission. In the 1990 swimsuit issue calendar, the senior editor writes that the models need "a ready recognition of the nature of the assignment, and a willingness to commit to it." An interviewed producer argues that *Sports Illustrated* selects photographers that "they can push around." The senior editor communicates her conceptions regarding meaning to others involved in the production of the issue. As one interviewed model describes it:

> Basically, when you do your first issue and your first shoot, and throughout the shooting, the [senior editor] . . . is constantly coaching you . . . as to what image they would like you to bring across . . . I sat down and sort of had an interview with *Sports Illustrated* before I even did the issue, and they told me what it was all about.

This model continued to note that if she was not "capturing" sensual meaning, producers "would say something."

The criteria producers use to select the backgrounds, swimwear, and models contributes to the consensus regarding the content of the issue. Some of the interviewed producers state that the locations for the pictures should include beaches, water, rocks, sky, and sunrises/sunsets. This routinization of the background encourages consumers to view the models as the most important part of the picture rather than the setting. Some of the interviewed producers note that *Sports Illustrated* often selects swimwear that "reveals" the models' bodies, and thus expresses sexual meaning. For example, one interviewed producer asserts that one of the "most important" criteria for selecting the swimwear is "sexuality." Producers consider "physical beauty" an important criteria to use when selecting the models. The interviewed producers believe that the beauty of the models is enhanced when they are thin, tall, "good" for swimwear, and adept at posing. In the modeling world, "good" for swimwear means more curvaceous than bodies used for modeling most other forms of clothing. As one interviewed producer describes it:

> *Sports Illustrated* does portray itself, and sells itself, on a tits-and-ass type issue. As a result, they're looking for curvy, curvaceous bodies, girls with good bodies, with tits and ass . . . They're looking for a model who is sexy, a model who can make a bathing suit look great.

Producers of the swimsuit issue use various posing, body management, and adornment techniques to create images which suggest meanings of ideal beauty to consumers. According to one interviewed producer, prior to the shoots the models tan in the nude and remove pubic hair. Letters from the Publisher indicate that the models use bleach to lighten their hair (1978) and cosmetics (1984). One of the interviewed models comments on the posing techniques:

> You just always have to be very conscious of how your body looks and how to sit and how not to sit, and how not to have your stomach out, and how not to have your thighs look too big in this position or that position . . . There's a definite technique as far as body movements.

Producers use the criteria of beauty to reduce the large number of photographs they take to the small number actually published. As one interviewed producer expresses it:

> You have to look for a flawless picture. [Flaws are] things like focus or a bad expression. Sometimes the flaws just happen to be the way a knee looks, or an arm looks, or an elbow, or just something that appears to be a blemish on the photograph, whether it's a shadow or one hair blowing in front of her eye.

Finally, the producers encourage interpretations of ideal beauty by touching up the pictures to remove signifiers[1] that run counter to the current beauty ideal. Some interviewed producers cite examples of aspects of swimsuit issue pictures producers touch up, including hair, wrinkles on a model's hip, color, dark shadows, and "funny positioning."

*Features of the Text*

Many components of the swimsuit issue texts encourage consumer consensus regarding the content and ideal readers of the issue. Of course, consumers need to attend to, and have particular understandings of, these features of textual structure for this process to work.

Some elements of the swimsuit issue texts suggest to the consumer that she/he should attend to the models' bodies. For example, the captions describe the models as alluring (1980; 1990), attracting attention (1986; 1987; 1989), and an eyeful (1989). The producers usually locate the models in the center of the pictures, and the bodies of the models typically fill up a large percentage of the space in the picture. Producers rarely crop the pictures above the model's mid-thigh. The swimsuit issues typically include pictures that do not present the swimwear in prominent ways, and pictures where the swimwear barely appears at all. The backgrounds behind the models look very routinized, and sometimes one cannot even see this background. The posing styles and expressions also suggest that consumers should focus on the bodies of the models. Many times the lower bodies of the models face one way, while their upper bodies and/or heads are twisted toward the spectator. In almost all of the pictures, the models pose with a head cant to the side and/or down, and eye aversion. Scholars argue that these conventions invite the spectator's guiltless gaze (e.g., Dyer, R., 1982; Goffman, 1976; Kuhn, 1985).

Many elements of the swimsuit issue texts urge consumers to view the models as ideally beautiful. For example, captions commonly suggest that the models epitomize beauty (e.g., 1970; 1976; 1984), and the title for the 1984 swimsuit spread was, "'A' You're Adorable, 'B' You're . . ." (pp. 64–65). The models featured in the swimsuit issue resemble the current feminine beauty ideal. For the most part, they are young, thin and curvaceous, lack blemishes, muscular definition and visible body hair (except on the scalp, eye area, and occasionally on the forearms), and show no signs of disability. The fact that the beauty ideal demands youthfulness and lack of disability is evidence that it reflects and reinforces ageism and ableism. Given the racism embedded in the dominant beauty ideal, it is not surprising that models of color have been underrepresented in the swimsuit issues over the years, almost all of the white models possess blonde or light brown, long and straight hair, and blue eyes prevail.

Many parts of the swimsuit issue texts encourage consumers to interpret the models as valid representatives of ideal femininity. People define femininity as clear difference from the masculine: women are or should be markedly dissimilar to men. The contrast between how women appear in the swimsuit issue and how men appear as athletes in *Sports Illustrated* accentuates such difference. On three occasions, the Letter from the Publisher has featured pictures of men posing like the women models.[2] Producers suggest that viewers perceive these pictures as humorous, probably because the pictured men represent a contrast to the models' femininity. The swimsuit issue texts commonly direct attention to the gender of the models. For example, a producer writing in the 1970 issue describes the swimwear as feminine, "...proving that girls can still resemble girls" (p. 34).

The physical characteristics of the models, described above, correspond with the current feminine appearance ideal. The fact that the models tend to resemble each other intimates that there is a single standard for ideal womanhood. The use of jewelry, cosmetics, and fashions with features such as lace and flowers also suggests that the models look feminine.

Since emotionality, connection to nature, lack of power, youthfulness, and (female) heterosexuality signify femininity in contemporary United States culture, the many features of the swimsuit issue texts that suggest these meanings encourage the consumer to associate the models with femininity. Some emotional activities attributed to the models in the captions are smoldering (1975), musing (1982), and being downcast (1989). When the written texts in the swimsuit issue feature a discussion of the models' status as wives and girlfriends (of men) these texts suggest that the models are heterosexual, a central component of the contemporary feminine ideal.

Poses, appearance management techniques, and swimwear featured in the swimsuit issue link the models to nature. Since the late 1970s, the swimsuit issues sometimes picture suits that resemble animal skins or plants. A recurring pose for models is a crawling position with the buttocks thrust upward, similar to the way many animals appear. Often in the 1980s, and occasionally in the 1970s, the swimsuit issue captions suggest that the suit or model resembles or blends in with parts of nature. Some routine appearance management or body decoration techniques insinuate meanings related to nature. For example, sometimes the hair of the models looks messy, suggesting natural freedom or disarray due to immersion in nature.

Many features of the swimsuit issue texts convey femininity by signifying in various ways that the models lack power. Their thinness and lack of muscular definition suggest that they lack physical power. The models also commonly pose in ways that express a lack of power (e.g., Berger, A., 1982; Goffman, 1976; Masse & Rosenblum, 1988). They rarely directly face the camera and often appear in a lying or crawling position, peering out from behind something, with their heads canted down and/or to the side, and with their eyes averted. Although most of the swimsuit issue pictures are shot from the same level as the model, the magazine published a significant number of pictures, especially in the 1980s and early 1990s, photographed from above the model.

Childhood also signifies a lack of power, and thus femininity. The lack of body hair on the models suggests that they resemble children. Poses that display immature movement patterns, silliness, and simple gymnastics moves encourage viewers to perceive the models as child-like. Other symbols of childhood, such as pigtails or ponytails, a child-like expression such as pouting, or a suit with a childlike theme, frequently accompany these poses. Childlikeness is also conveyed through written texts in the swimsuit issue. For example, the Letter from the Publisher often portrays the models as innocent and frightened. One publisher writes about a model bringing a stuffed animal along for security (1985); another describes a model as bridging "the gap between the innocent little girl look and the sophisticated woman look" (1976, p. 6).

Femininity is not a politically neutral construct. The notions that women are vastly different from men, overly emotional, childlike, physically weak, dependent on men, and connected to nature (rather than civilization) have been used to limit women's power. Thus, when *Sports Illustrated* publishes images that reinforce these ideas about women, they reinforce sexism.

Many parts of the swimsuit issue texts encourage consumers to think that the issue conveys sexual meaning. Youthfulness, thinness, curvaceousness, hairless bodies, long blonde scalp hair, and cosmetics are widely-accepted contemporary signifiers of a woman's (passive) sexual appeal. In the West, due to the racist stereotype that people of color are licentious, dark skin signifies unrestrained sexuality; therefore the tanned skin of the white models increases the perception that they are sexy (Lurie, 1981; Urry, 1990).

Many consumers think that the swimwear pictured in the swimsuit issue contributes to the sexual meaning of the issue. For example, one interviewed consumer calls the swimwear "erotic." Although diverse styles of bathing suits appear in the swimsuit issue, suits with features that suggest sexual meaning appear regularly. Since people in the

United States generally perceive breasts, buttocks, and the pubic area as erogenous zones, and nudity itself as sexual, they associate outfits which expose most of the body or these parts of the body with sexuality. The material, style, and size of the suits appearing in the swimsuit issues reveal the contours and edges of these erogenous zones, especially since the 1970s. Some examples of swimwear featured in *Sports Illustrated* that suggest nakedness include: [white] flesh colored suits, suits without tops, suits with see-through parts, suits with minimal material, and suits with large v-cut openings down the middle of the chest. Written texts in the swimsuit issue commonly reinforce this sexual meaning. For example, captions from the 1970s and 1980s intimate that the models are stripped (1977; 1985), wearing no top (1971; 1979; 1982; 1983), and almost wearing or barely wearing a suit (1979; 1980; 1982; 1983).

Many consumers feel that the posing featured in the swimsuit issue conveys sexual meaning. For example, one interviewed consumer describes the poses as "sexually oriented." The models usually arch and cant their bodies, which creates a curvaceous look, thus signifying sexuality. In the 1980s and early 1990s, the models sometimes hold parts of their suits in ways that reveal more of their bodies or suggest that they might reveal more. Two facial expressions that signify sexual meaning, the come-on and autoerotic look, often appear in the swimsuit issues. Models create the come-on look by slightly parting their lips, looking at the camera with narrowed eyes, and tilting their heads to the side (and perhaps downward) so that they glance at the camera in a slightly angled way. When constructing an autoerotic look, the model tilts her head fully backwards, slightly parts her lips, and closes or narrows her eyes (e.g., Coward, 1985; Kuhn, 1985; Millum, 1975).

Finally, the swimsuit issue texts suggest that the ideal readers of the issue are men and boys. For example, the Letter from the Publisher in 1976 implies that the swimsuit issue models appeal more to men than women; the publisher states that one of these models " . . . may not be the girl all women want to look like, but she has a quality that makes her the way most men think a woman should look" (p. 6). The author of an article in the 1989 anniversary swimsuit issue discusses how young men use the swimsuit issue pictures as pin-up material.

*Schooling the Reader*

Through their references to the swimsuit issue in media texts other than the spread itself, *Sports Illustrated* producers encourage the denotative level meaning consensus, and thus end up schooling readers about "appropriate" interpretations of the issue. For example, some recent television advertisements for *Sports Illustrated* that are explicitly aimed at men highlight the swimsuit issue, linking it with male consumers. The titles producers place above the published letters of reader response to the swimsuit issue nurture the consensus. These titles commonly suggest that consumers should direct their attention to the bodies of the models, such as "Fore and Hindsight" (January 26, 1969), to the beauty of the models, such as "Bathing Beauties" (January 30, 1978), or to the sexuality of the models, such as "Uncover Girl" (February 1, 1965).

Several parts of the 1989 swimsuit issue video encourage consumers to define the content of the issue as ideally beautiful and sexy women's bodies. For example, the producers describe one model as sexy, and then the video pictures her stating that models need to "flirt with the camera." The producers highlight body parts that signify sexuality by focusing the camera on these parts and zooming slowly up or down the body. For example, in one segment, a model pulls a tank top up to reveal the lower part of her breasts as the camera operator zooms in on her chest and the photographer says, "Come a little closer to me, Elle. Now pull it over your head. Go for it."

*The Social Context*

In order for consumers to see women's bodies, femininity, ideal beauty, and sexuality as the central content of the swimsuit issue, they must be familiar with the signifiers of these meanings that appear in the swimsuit issues. For example, one must understand the normative signifiers of women's sexuality, such as curvaceousness and the come-on facial expression, to interpret the swimsuit issue as conveying sexual meaning. Since normative signifiers of beauty, femininity, and sexuality regularly appear in the mass media in the United States, consumers typically have learned the common meaning of these signifiers.

The social context also encourages consumers to believe that the swimsuit issue is designed for men. In United States culture *Sports Illustrated* magazine itself is typically associated with men, and this bolsters the notion that the swimsuit issue is aimed at men. One interviewed consumer explicitly calls *Sports Illustrated* a "men's magazine," while another consumer explains:

> I think that mainly men are probably interested in [*Sports Illustrated*]. I would guess they would be [the] main subscribers. And,

therefore, [with the swimsuit issue] they're gearing more toward them by putting out an issue they would be interested in.

The wider societal context also socializes people to believe that heterosexuality is natural, universal, and compelling, and thus most people in the United States take this belief for granted. If consumers assume that the issue signifies sexual meaning and that all readers are heterosexual, then they often deduce that producers make the issue for men. For example, one interviewed consumer notes, "The male audience would be attracted to women in swimsuits ... The issues I've seen, they didn't have any men in bikinis. Therefore, they're definitely not catering to a female audience." Another interviewed consumer argues:

> The whole idea behind *Sports Illustrated* [swimsuit issue] is sexual ... A man probably ... would not be as likely to pick up a [women's] fashion magazine and look at [their] swimsuit issue ... [But] they would [look at] *Sports Illustrated* [swimsuit issue].

## Recognizing the Power of Producers and the Text

Although audience members hold a variety of disparate opinions about the swimsuit issue, it is clear that the intentions of producers, production practices, the swimsuit issue texts, media texts other than the swimsuit issue, and the wider sociocultural context all contribute to consumer consensus regarding the denotative level meaning of the swimsuit issue. These findings illustrate the point that there are many factors that affect the audience during the process of interpretation. The intentions of producers and various parts of the production process clearly influence the structure and content of media texts. The structure and content of media texts just as clearly influence the meanings consumers produce when they interact with the texts.

Yet, textual structure alone cannot prompt a consumer to decode a media text in a manner that matches the producer's intentions. The cultural knowledge/perspective that the consumer employs during decoding must, to a large degree, correspond with that of the producers for consumers to create a dominant/preferred reading of the text (e.g., Lewis, 1991; Morley, 1980; Woollacott, 1982; Wren-Lewis, 1983). In fact, effective communication depends on some correspondence between encoded and decoded meanings (Condit, 1989; Hall, 1984). It appears that a common cultural setting often provides producers and consumers with a similar understanding of many symbols, and this similar understanding limits the potential for resistant readings on the part of consumers.

Justin Lewis (1991) argues that the ideological[3] power of the mass media does not depend on producers' intentions. He also maintains that the polysemic nature of media texts does not diminish the ideological power of the media.[4] I have no reason to doubt these claims. But, the results of my scholarship on the swimsuit issue lead me to conclude that producers' intentions and practices, and textual structure, do influence the ideological power of the media. The way producers shape the content and structure of media texts does influence consumer interpretations. Within a given cultural context, textual content and structure set the stage for debates over meaning. As the normative meaning of signifiers change, interpretations of content will change. But, the consumer still must work with texts that represent a limited number of signifiers.

The findings of this study provide a crucial warning against the recent trend in media studies to grant practically unlimited power to the audience and dismiss the producers and texts as barely relevant. The fact that producers influence the interpretations of many consumers, through the ways they shape textual content and structure, suggests that attempts to critique and change media texts may be one useful strategy for affecting wider social change.

# The Struggle over Public Sexuality

Despite the power of producers to encourage preferred readings in a given cultural context through the ways they shape media texts, consumers produce different interpretations of these texts. The popular media serve as a site of ideological struggle, where groups strive to influence which meanings circulate and predominate in society and thus where consent for hegemony can be won or lost (e.g., Bennett, 1986; Curran, Gurevitch & Woollacott, 1982; Hall, 1977).

The swimsuit issue serves as a centerpiece for an ideological struggle. Most people in the United States, including most of the interviewed consumers and producers, are aware of this struggle. As one interviewed consumer puts it, "You can just say those two words [swimsuit issue], and everybody's got their opinion."

Thirty-eight of the thirty-nine interviewed consumers voiced a discernable opinion of the swimsuit issue: about twenty-five percent have a neutral (i.e., indifferent) opinion, about thirty percent find it enjoyable due to its portrayal of sexuality and/or beauty, and about forty-five percent criticize it. Of those who criticize it, about ten percent of the interviewed consumers disapprove of the swimsuit issue only because they think it should not appear in a sports magazine, about ten percent due to its sexual focus, and about twenty-five percent because they view it as sexist. In addition to these readings, one of the interviewed consumers enjoys the swimsuit issue for its portrayal of fashion trends and role models, one disapproves of the issue because he views it as racist, and a few criticize the issue because they see it as a sensationalized sales gimmick.

These diverse readings of the swimsuit issue stem from the fact that consumers use a variety of perspectives to decode the text. Twenty-six percent of the interviewed consumers indicate that they changed their views about the swimsuit issue over the years, and most of these consumers attribute the change to new experiences that altered their belief system. A variety of sociocultural factors produce their different belief systems. These factors include different locations in a stratification system (e.g., race and sexual orientation) and different experiences (e.g., those that stem from attending college or a particular occupation).

The debate surrounding the swimsuit issue primarily focuses on the topics of gender and sexuality. Most people know that the conflict revolves around these topics. Issues of race, nationality, and economics have a significant impact on this debate, but most people do not perceive these three issues as central to the public conflict. This chapter addresses the struggle over sexual meaning. Future chapters deal with gender, race, nationality, and economics.

### Debating the Degree of Sexual Meaning

Pictures do not contain intrinsic sexual meanings, as these meanings emerge from the interaction of factors such as pictorial codes/conventions, captions, the perspectives viewers bring to decoding, and the context in which consumers interpret the pictures. Consumers only interpret signifiers as expressing sexual meaning if they have previously learned, through the wider culture and contact with other media texts, to associate these signifiers with this meaning (e.g., Ferran, 1987; Kuhn, 1985; Lewallen, 1988).

Although most consumers view the content of the swimsuit issue as sexual, they hold different opinions about the degree of sexual meaning expressed by the issue. Some label the swimsuit issue pornography and see it as featuring explicit sexual meaning. For example, one interviewed consumer describes the issue as "a version of *Playboy*" and " . . . a sexually motivated enterprise." Other interviewed consumers feel that the issue presents sexual meaning in more subtle ways. One interviewed consumer articulates this view when he says that the swimsuit issue:

> . . . doesn't really [fit] onto the pornographic or the exploitation side. It's on the sensual side, but it kind of pushes that. It's kind of like trashy TV shows, in a way, that sort of hint at something, but don't actually come right out and show.

It is no surprise that audience members have contradictory opinions about the degree of sexual meaning expressed by the swimsuit issue. Many elements of production, the swimsuit issue texts, and the social context help fuel this debate.

*Features of Production That Contribute to this Debate*

Some of the interviewed swimsuit issue producers have as their aim to express explicit sexual meaning, while others hope to communicate very subtle sensual meaning. Whereas one interviewed producer states that the swimsuit issue is not designed as "a *Playboy* type thing," another declares that it is "there to sell sex." Most of the interviewed producers hope to communicate a subtle, tasteful, and classy form of eroticism. As one interviewed producer maintains, unlike "a really sleazy magazine," the swimsuit issue pictures are designed to express "a certain element of taste," being "sexy without being lewd."

Several of the interviewed producers, like Deford (1989), say that the senior editor monitors the degree of sexual meaning expressed in the swimsuit issue, working to ensure that none of the other producers encode "explicit sexuality." However, other producers intend to express more explicit sexual meaning. So, it is likely that the producers shape the texts in ways that reflect a struggle over the degree of sexual meaning. An interviewed photographer describes an example of such a struggle, saying that the senior editor "is very, very protective of the girls" when he tries to encode "sexuality."

The criteria employed to select the producers of the swimsuit issue helps *Sports Illustrated* to convey more subtle sexual meaning. Interviewed producers indicate that they attempt to select photographers who will create pictures that express the appropriate "image of the swimsuit issue." They hire models who symbolize "wholesomeness" and the "girl-next-door" look. In addition, as one interviewed model describes it, the models:

> ... have to be able to be professional [and] uphold the image of *Sports Illustrated*, because that's what's at stake, you know ... If you have someone out there ... who's not upholding a positive image ... it's going to sort of bring the respectable value of the swimsuit issue down ... When they're picking a young woman [model], they're not going to pick someone who's going to put the reputation of *Sports Illustrated* at jeopardy.

Obviously, *Sports Illustrated* is going to attempt to avoid hiring models who work for the pornography industry.

In regard to degree of sexual meaning, it is likely that some parts of the swimsuit issue texts reflect the interests of some producers while other parts of these texts reflect the interests of other producers. In this case, consumers may have different views about the degree of sexual meaning because they focus on different parts of the text. Or, perhaps the struggle among producers results in a text that consistently delivers subtle sexual meaning. This might inspire the disagreements over the degree of sexual meaning, as some consumers focus on the mere presence of sexual signifiers while others focus on the "subtle nature" of these signifiers. It is clear that production practices result in somewhat "open" texts that allow for multiple interpretations regarding the degree of sexual meaning.

*Features of the Texts That Contribute to this Debate*

The photographs in the swimsuit issue contain a mixture of signifiers that leave the text open to a wide range of interpretations regarding the degree of sexual meaning expressed.[1] Some of the pictures contain many conventions that signify sexuality while other pictures feature few of these conventions. The fact that the majority of the pictures contain a small number of subtle sexual conventions, rather than a large number of explicit sexual conventions or no sexual conventions at all, encourages the interpretation that the texts express a "subtle" form of sexuality. The swimsuit issue pictures expose parts of erogenous zones and consumers can see erogenous zones through a light covering, but the pictures never fully expose the models. The producers mix pictures of "well-covered" models with pictures of models who wear little clothing. When the models wear particularly revealing clothing their poses often lack sexual signifiers, whereas when the models wear clothing that does not symbolize sexual meaning their poses often signify sexuality. The hairless bodies of the models and their childlike poses may suggest childlike innocence, in contrast to the more explicit sexuality signalled in other ways. Elements of the swimsuit issue texts that express meanings related to travel, athleticism, and fashion discourage the interpretation that the issue denotes purely sexual meaning.

The words of *Sports Illustrated* producers in media texts other than the swimsuit spread suggest, over and over, that the swimsuit issue expresses sexual meaning in a tasteful and classy manner. For example, in the 1989 swimsuit issue video, comments by two of the models intimate that they possess a great deal of modesty. The author of an article in the 1989 25th anniversary swimsuit issue reports that models want to pose for the swimsuit issue because they feel that the senior editor never makes them "look salacious" (Deford, 1989, p. 44).

### How Genre Plays a Part in this Debate

The swimsuit issue bears some resemblance to representations classified in the genres of pin-ups, pornography, art, and advertising. If consumers could categorize the swimsuit issue within the genre of pornography, advertising, or art, this would suggest a more fixed degree of sexual meaning, but multiple factors discourage easy categorization.

If the swimsuit issue clearly fit into the pornographic genre, consumers would probably see it as more sexually explicit, yet several factors dissuade consumers from interpreting the swimsuit issue as pornographic. The presence of the swimsuit issue spread in a sports magazine discourages consumers from categorizing the spread as pornography. Consumers know that production and consumption of sports magazines differ from production and consumption of pornographic texts. A specialized industry which operates outside of mainstream media realms creates, markets, and distributes most pornography. The public, including children, have easy access to sports magazines, including *Sports Illustrated,* furthering the perception that the sexual representation in the swimsuit spread must be subtle/tasteful and thus non-pornographic. In fact, some consumers believe that many boys and men prefer the swimsuit issue over pornography because it is located in a sports magazine and thus appears more socially acceptable. As one interviewed consumer explains:

> If the average male, let's say a married male, in particular, dragged home an issue of *Playboy*, there'd be a lot of women who'd say, "Get it out of the house." But if you bring it home in a *Sports Illustrated* magazine . . . it would be maybe considered acceptable.

Another interviewed consumer states:

> It's like soft pornography, only they're using the title "*Sports Illustrated*" . . . [Men] can get it and still be politically correct and say, "Well, I don't look at it, it just sort of comes with the subscription." You know, as opposed to having to go out and buying a *Penthouse* . . . [The readers] can have it without actually,

you know, owning [up to] it. It's like having a book of naked women with the *Good Housekeeping* seal of approval or something.

The widespread use of representations of curvaceous women in swimwear in United States (non-pornographic) popular culture also discourages the pornographic interpretation. The fact that producers use reputable fashion models in the swimsuit issue, rather than models from the pornography industry, advances the interpretation that the issue represents sexuality in a tasteful manner. Finally, the fact that the swimsuit issue models do wear some clothes discourages consumers from defining the issue as pornography.

On the other hand, some factors encourage consumers to link the swimsuit issue with the pornographic genre. The fact that some conventions common in pornography regularly appear in the swimsuit issue, such as representing women on their own with the come-on and autoerotic looks, may foster this view. It is common knowledge that boys/men often consume the swimsuit issue in isolation or with other boys/men, which is similar to how many men consume pornography (Buchbinder, 1987; Brod, 1984; Hite, 1981; Kappeler, 1986). Many people think that part of a boy's experience of growing up and learning about sexuality involves viewing pornography (Root, 1984). Boys often consume the swimsuit issue as part of a rite of passage into adult sexuality. The common knowledge that some people react to the sexual meaning of the swimsuit issue by canceling their subscriptions to *Sports Illustrated* and censoring the swimsuit issue suggest a link to the pornographic genre. The notion that the *Sports Illustrated* swimsuit issue is related to the genre of pornography was recently confirmed for me, because soon after I started ordering *Sports Illustrated* swimsuit issue calendars through the mail I began to receive advertisements for *Playboy* in the mail. I suspect that I started receiving these advertisements because *Sports Illustrated* shared its mailing list with *Playboy*, since advertisements for *Playboy* and the swimsuit issue calendars are the only two items I receive in the mail that are addressed to "L. Davis." The fact that the swimsuit issue resembles pornography in some ways enhances the sexual meaning of the issue.

Although some factors suggest that the swimsuit issue expresses artistic meaning, resembling the common icon of nude women in "high art," other factors discourage this interpretation.[2] Thus, the swimsuit issue can tap, but cannot fully draw on, an aura of artistic respectability that would help to define the swimsuit issue as a tasteful form of sexual representation. The location of the swimsuit issue spread in a sports magazine deters consumers from categorizing the spread as art, because they usually do not think of sports magazines as featuring representations of art. The production and consumption of sports magazines differ from art production and consumption. Art producers offer a limited number of editions of artistic texts, and they market these texts to a relatively exclusive audience (Kappeler, 1986; Rosenblum, 1978), whereas production and consumption of sport magazines and the swimsuit issue take place on a mass scale. On the other hand, the producers identify the swimsuit issue photographer in the text, and many of the swimsuit issue pictures look technically perfect and involve technical innovation, two factors encouraging consumers to view the swimsuit spread as art.

Poe (1976) and Duquin (1989) observe that images of women in swimwear commonly appear in advertising, especially advertising designed to express sexual meaning. If consumers could clearly define the spread as advertisement, this would suggest limited sexual meaning.

Features of the swimsuit issue texts that induce consumers to define the swimsuit spread as an article, rather than as advertising, include identifying the spread in the table of contents, naming the author/editor and photographer of the spread, and highlighting the spread on the cover of the magazine. Common knowledge that the pleasure many consumers derive from the swimsuit issue does not depend on the purchase of another commodity also discourages consumers from defining the spread as advertising. Producers structure advertisements in ways that offer future pleasure to audience members. As Meyers (1982a) explains:

> Crucially, for the image to fulfill its advertising function, it must not offer satisfaction in its own right. The advertisement works to displace satisfaction, promising fulfillment upon the purchase of the commodity, at which point the reader becomes consumer. (p. 90)

On the other hand, the swimsuit spread names the prices and manufacturers/designers of the swimwear, as an advertisement might. Also, the producers do not accept advertisements that too closely resemble the swimsuit spread, due to their concern that consumers might confuse the advertisements with the spread itself. Lastly, if consumers are aware of the fact that some consumers do purchase the swimwear featured in the swimsuit issue, this might move them to view the issue as advertising.

The swimsuit issue can be classified within the genre of pin-ups. Gabor (1973) usefully defines pin-ups as:

. . . a sexually evocative image, reproduced in multiple copies, in which either the expression or attitude of the subject invites the viewer to participate vicariously in or fantasize about personal involvement with the subject. (p. 17)

Pin-ups commonly appear on posters, postcards, and calendars, and in pornographic, Hollywood, and so-called men's magazines. One does not need to take a representation out of a magazine for it to fit the definition of pin-up (Gabor, 1973).

Kuhn (1985) argues that pin-ups remain open to more diverse interpretations than pornography, because often pornography more directly suggests sexual meaning through fragmentation of bodies and greater sexual explicitness. Pin-up models are commonly partially clad. Women pin-up models usually possess curvaceous bodies and relatively large breasts, and pin-up pictures often partly or fully expose the breasts (Gabor, 1973). Because pin-ups often lack more explicit signifiers of sexual meaning, producers of pin-ups often use come-on facial expressions to suggest sexual meaning (Kuhn, 1985).

Pin-ups of women in swimsuits or in (other) sexually fetishized clothing are common and have been popular for many years. Early on, general magazines and sport magazines included representations of women in swimsuits. The early *Life* magazine introduced images of the Gibson Girl, a woman who conformed to normative standards of beauty and who sometimes appeared in swimwear, and other magazines soon imitated these images (Breazeale, 1994; Gabor, 1973).

Boys/men consume pin-ups of women in many different ways. They usually view pin-ups in isolation or with other boys/men in settings which primarily boys/men inhabit, such as locker rooms, dorm rooms, and male-dominated factories. Women in these settings sometimes view the pin-ups as harassment (Gabor, 1973; Hearn, 1985; Root, 1984). Men often fantasize about sexual relations with the pictured model, or about how association with the model would bestow status upon them. Together, men sometimes boast about how they could perform with the pictured models (Gabor, 1973).

Several factors encourage the interpretation that the pictures from the swimsuit issue make good pin-up material. First, as already discussed, the poses and expressions of the swimsuit issue models encourage consumers to see them as spectacle. Second, producers make the swimsuit issue pictures relatively large, which enables the use of these pictures as posters. Third, the swimsuit issue pictures tend to resemble, on a smaller scale, posters of women in swimwear that many stores offer for sale. Fourth, the fact that *Sports Illustrated* sells calendars with pictures from the swimsuit issue suggests that consumers should view the issue as poster material. Finally, many people possess the knowledge that some consumers use the swimsuit issue pictures as pin-up material.

My interviews with librarians furnish one indication that consumers view the swimsuit issue as pin-up material, in that people remove pictures from the issue in, and steal the issue from, many libraries. Later, I discuss other ways that consumers use the swimsuit issue pictures as pin-ups.

The many factors that encourage consumers to interpret the swimsuit issue as pin-up material do not help to produce consensus among consumers regarding the degree of sexual meaning exhibited by the issue. This is because consumers often disagree with each other about the degree of sexual meaning expressed by texts from the pin-up genre (Kuhn, 1985).

## *Debating the Morality of Public Displays of Sexuality*

Consumers' debates about the sexual meaning of the swimsuit issue go beyond the degree of sexual meaning the issue conveys. The swimsuit issue serves as a catalyst for a debate regarding the morality of representing sexuality.

### *Public Displays of Sexuality as Immoral*

Some consumers disapprove of sexual representation, and because they think the swimsuit issue features sexual representation they view the issue as immoral. For example, one interviewed consumer argues that the swimsuit issue is a problem "because of the brevity of the swimsuits." A 1983 letter to the editor from "the Art Collins Family" says that:

> We do not approve of pornography in any form . . . This issue was nothing more than smut . . . We don't patronize such things: we don't have cable T.V. and we don't go to R-rated movies, because we choose not to. However, you have taken that choice away . . . (February 28, p. 80)

According to those who create this reading, the swimsuit issue and other forms of sexual representation degrade women by tarnishing their reputations and corrupt boys by pushing them into premature sexual relationships. One interviewed consumer comments that the phenomenon of "women exposing themselves" in the swimsuit issue is "downgrading to women." A letter printed in *Sports Illustrated* reads:

> It is . . . sad to see *SI,* which so often takes the moral high ground, increasingly pander to its readers' lusts . . . Do you even think, for example, of the thousands of teenage boys who read your magazine religiously? Would to God you had any interest in preserving their chastity. (February 25, 1985, pp. 75–76)

Consumers who read the swimsuit issue in this way view sexuality as a private matter, and public signifiers of sexual meaning as immoral. They also think that consumption of sexual representations is a stepping stone toward actual sexual relations. They think that adolescent sexuality is immoral, that people should avoid sexual experiences until adulthood (and probably until marriage).

Those who criticize the swimsuit issue for its sexual meaning often attempt to censor the issue in some way. As evident from letters printed in *Sports Illustrated,* these individuals sometimes cancel their subscription to the magazine, throw away the swimsuit issue, or remove the swimsuit spread from the magazine. My interviews with librarians furnish evidence that some librarians, especially those who work in libraries that primarily serve children, confiscate the swimsuit issue, choosing not to place the issue in the library. Other librarians keep the swimsuit issue in the library but do not display it, either placing it behind a monitored desk or concealing the location of the issue and only revealing this location upon request.

Consumers who articulate this reading of the swimsuit issue build on the denotative level meaning that the issue expresses sexual meaning. Furthermore, these consumers typically focus on elements of the swimsuit issue that suggest more explicit sexual meaning, and thus they usually argue that the issue conveys pornographic meaning.

The fact that producers acknowledge the existence of this reading in *Sports Illustrated* increases the likelihood that consumers would be familiar with this interpretation. For example, sometimes when *Sports Illustrated* producers discuss the overall impact of the swimsuit issue they mention this reading, and producers often publish letters that articulate it.

In the United States, the popularity of conservative views regarding sexuality and the display of sexuality make this oppositional reading relatively common. Negative reactions to the pro-sex movement of the 1960s and 1970s, and attempts to censor sexual images, by the religious right wing have intensified in the last decade. Yet, for consumers to create this reading their commitment to these conservative views must be strong enough to enable them to ignore or reject textual suggestions that males should enjoy the swimsuit issue, that the issue contains tasteful representations of sexuality, and that consumers should perceive the issue in a lighthearted manner.

### Enjoying the Sexuality and Having Fun
### Defying "the Prudes"

One reason many consumers enjoy the swimsuit issue is because they enjoy representations of sexuality. The interviewed consumers connect their appreciation of the swimsuit issue to its sexual meaning in a variety of ways. For example, one interviewed consumer says that what he likes about the swimsuit issue is the models' "big chests" and "tans." When asked if this means that he enjoys the sexual display, he responds affirmatively. When another interviewed consumer explains why he likes the swimsuit issue he remarks, "I already admitted that I purchase *Playboy* magazine;" thus he ties his interest in sexual images to his enjoyment of the issue. Some of the interviewed male consumers only indirectly imply that they appreciate the sexual meaning of the swimsuit issue. For example, these consumers sometimes state that they enjoy the issue, and that men [in general] like the issue because of its representation of sexuality. The current social climate, where many people condemn those who admit an interest in sexual representation, probably contributes to the hesitancy of these consumers to declare directly that they enjoy sexual meaning, especially since they had no idea what I think of sexual representation.

Many consumers who enjoy the swimsuit issue for its sexual meaning define people who are morally opposed to the sexual character of the swimsuit issue as "prudes." Most often, "moral police-like" figures (e.g., religious figures), institutional authorities (e.g., librarians and teachers), and women are accused of this prudishness. For example, one letter to the editor from 1970 reads:

I enjoy reading the letters that you publish two weeks [after publication of the swimsuit issue] from overprotective mothers and repressive librarians who threaten to cancel their subscriptions because of the 'obscene' pictures. Keep up the good work! (January 26, p. 62)

Consumers who enjoy the swimsuit issue often frame the debate over the public display of sexuality as a war between men and women, labeling women, especially mothers and wives, as too puritanical and controlling. In 1984, *Sports Illustrated* printed a letter from a man who states that, "It seems women lead the antiswimsuit faction, claiming it corrupts children and degrades women" (March 12, p. 86). One interviewed consumer argues that objection to the sexual display in the swimsuit issue ". . . usually [comes] from mothers [who] . . . are afraid of their sons seeing this at too early an age."

According to many consumers who enjoy the swimsuit issue, censorship of the issue is an anti-American act. For example, one letter writer compliments *Sports Illustrated* for continuing to print both the swimsuit issue and letters that criticize the issue, saying that these practices " . . . exemplify the freedom and integrity that are the foundation of this great nation" (March 12, 1984, p. 84).

Many of the consumers who appreciate the sexual character of the swimsuit issue seem to derive great pleasure from defying those who object to the sexual content. Some Letters to the Editor suggest that many men enjoy reading, hiding, and/or defending the swimsuit issue partly because women and authority figures in their lives view it as taboo. For example, in 1985 a letter writer states:

Each year I await the letters responding to the swimsuit issue as eagerly as I wait for the issue itself. I have to laugh at the cries of 'Pornography!' and 'Cancel my subscription!' (February 25, p. 76)

On March 3, 1986, *Sports Illustrated* printed a letter from a man who says that his wife made him write a letter objecting to the swimsuit issue, but then he asks *Sports Illustrated* to continue to send him the issue disguised as *Ladies Home Companion.*

Articles written by *Sports Illustrated* producers sometimes encourage readers to enjoy the controversy generated by the swimsuit issue and to take some delight in defying those who object to the issue on sexual grounds. For example, the authors of a couple of articles in the 1989 anniversary swimsuit issue encourage consumers to view censorship of the issue (especially by women) as both prudish and fruitless. Of course, those who make fun of "the prudes" always have the last word, as *Sports Illustrated* continues to publish the swimsuit issue.

The popularity of the swimsuit issue must be seen in the context of centuries of sexual repression in Western societies. This repression has severely limited the live and mediated sexual experiences of people in Western countries. In the United States, we have few opportunities to consume sexual representations in public to resist the current climate of sexual repression, because consumption of these representations is often legally and normatively restricted to private spaces. Yet, because the swimsuit issue is published by a sports magazine and signifies sexuality in a somewhat subtle manner, it can be consumed in a more public manner. The fact that most view the swimsuit issue as a text about sexuality allows people to consume it in public in ways that convey resistance against those who favor continued repression of our sexual lives. Thus, the popularity of the swimsuit issue is probably enhanced by the fact that it is a useful tool for taking a public stand against sexual repression.

Viewing the swimsuit issue as a tool one can use to resist sexual repression explains the energetic antagonism consumers of the swim-suit issue often direct at institutional authorities and "moral police-like" figures. People who occupy these roles often serve as symbolic representatives or enforcers of repressive sexual policies.

Although many women participate in the anti-sexuality movement in the United States and thus some women are legitimate targets for those who resist sexual repression, clearly too much of the blame for sexual repression has been laid on women's shoulders. The many men who equate anti-sexuality criticism of the swimsuit issue with women do not understand the difference between anti-sexuality and (pro-sex) feminist readings of the swimsuit issue.

*A Pro-Sex Feminist Viewpoint*

Some feminists who criticize the swimsuit issue do not object to the representation of sexuality. Four of the interviewed consumers who view the swimsuit issue as sexist made a point of saying that they do not disapprove of all forms of sexual representation. For example, one of these consumers claims that she is "not generally opposed to soft-core pornography." Another interviewed consumer declared that she is "not a prude," and maintains that if the swimsuit issue featured sexual images of men along with the sexual images of women, then she would "pay up there with the rest of them" and give her "sign of approval to the magazine."

Some feminists criticize the tendencies of other feminists to equate sexual representation with sexism, maintaining that sexual representation is not inherently sexist. Some feminist scholars argue that fragmentation and objectification of the body in sexual representation is not inherently demeaning or sexist. All visual representations objectify (Betterton, 1987; Weir & Casey, 1984). As Weir and Casey (1984) point out, "The material nature of representations necessitates their presentation as objects for other people" (p. 144). And, as Meyers (1982b) contends, people must fragment and objectify aspects of the complex world to make it meaningful. Weir and Casey (1984) argue that sexuality necessitates objectification, because it involves interaction with the materiality of other bodies and their particular characteristics.

The debate about the public display of sexuality that surrounds the swimsuit issue is a difficult one for feminists to enter. Feminists who take either side in this debate end up aligning themselves with conservative forces who oppose many feminist goals. Feminists who oppose the swimsuit issue because it features sexual display find themselves in the same camp as the religious right wing. And if feminists were to side with consumers of the swimsuit issue who defend the sexual display, then they would align themselves with many individuals who pursue versions of masculinity that buttress sexism. Feminists can avoid this difficulty by stating that while much pleasure can be derived from consensual sex and representations of sexuality, the swimsuit issue nevertheless reflects and reinforces sexism. In other words, feminists can articulate the position that although representations of sexuality are not inherently immoral or shameful, *Sports Illustrated* offers a version of sexuality that is rooted in sexist assumptions.

# A Vehicle for Public Declarations of Heterosexual Identity

Why does *Sports Illustrated* stray from its usual diet of sports coverage to display images that most define as sexual? This chapter provides the foundation for an answer to this question. Here, I narrow my discussion of sexuality to what I see as the central meaning of the swimsuit issue, heterosexuality.

## It's about Heterosexuality

People in the United States are embedded in social contexts that are saturated with the message that heterosexuality is natural, universal, and compelling. Texts produced by *Sports Illustrated* reflect and reinforce this assumption by encouraging consumers to believe that men and adolescent boys are naturally attracted to the swimsuit issue. For example, in the Letter from the Publisher in the 1974 swimsuit issue, the publisher describes the models sunbathing in the nude while delighted workmen strain to catch occasional glimpses. The 1987 swimsuit issue contains an article about women's swimsuit fashion, in which the author depicts men as "peeping toms" who desire to look at women in revealing swimwear. The authors of a couple of articles in the 1989 25th anniversary swimsuit issue suggest that young men, who are moving through hormonally-prompted stages from boyhood to manhood, make a transition from primarily valuing pin-ups of men athletic heroes to valuing sexualized pin-ups of women.

The fact that the swimsuit issue texts represent women in ways that most interpret as expressing sexual meaning, along with textual suggestions that nature compels men and older boys to pursue such spectacle, suggest a heterosexual ideal subject position.[1] Thus, the swim-suit issue texts beckon heterosexual male readers.[2]

Most consumer interpretations of the swimsuit issue take this ideal subject position into account. The assumption of natural, universal, and compelling heterosexuality moves many consumers to claim that there is a direct relationship between one's gender and one's opinion of the issue. Consumers often argue that men enjoy the issue, whereas women either hold a neutral or oppositional opinion. As one interviewed con-sumer expresses this, "The male reader . . . looks forward to [the swim-suit issue] . . . [whereas] your average female . . . probably looks at these magazines and they either scorn them or they say 'Well, big deal.'" Another interviewed consumer comments, "I can see a male buying it before a female buying it."

Consumers often state that men are naturally attracted to looking at the swimsuit issue. For example, one interviewed consumer says that men like the swimsuit issue because "men like women and women like men." When another interviewed consumer said that "males are going to, of course, be attracted" to the swimsuit issue, I asked him if "all males" possess this interest. He responded by saying, "Whether they want to admit it, I'd say they are to a certain extent, sure. I mean, that's what makes the world go 'round, the birds and bees."

Many consumers believe that adolescent boys are especially drawn to the swimsuit issue and other images of "sexy women" because they are moving through natural stages of sexual development which in-volve the discovery and exploration of physical sexual differences between women and men, and then sexual attraction to women. An interviewed consumer makes this point when he says that, when "you're just a little kid and growing up and discovering things for the first time" the women in the swimsuit issue are "legal" "sexual fantasies." Another interviewed consumer states, " . . . having two sons, I realize that [being drawn to looking at the swimsuit issue] is just kind of a part of human nature, I guess." This consumer views the swimsuit issue and pornogra-phy as a natural curiosity for boys, who have "their horizons expanding," and who are coming "to realize that there is a distinction between boys and girls, and women like his mother and women [with] big bahoomgas."

Although most consumers make the assumption that heterosexual-ity compels male interest in the swimsuit issue, consumers rarely explic-itly mention heterosexuality. Yet, one interviewed gay male consumer responded to a question as to why many men like the issue by stating, "It's because they're straight males that think that it's really neat that they get an issue of very scantily clothed women with their *Sports Illustrated*."

Only one of the thirty-nine interviewed consumers questions the assumption that only heterosexual men appreciate the sexual meaning of the swimsuit issue. This consumer, a girl who describes her parents and upbringing as "liberal," argues that the swimsuit issue "provides a totally legal way for men, or women, depending, to get their kicks."

The words of many consumers imply that their own (hetero)sexual orientation shapes their view of the swimsuit issue. Many male consumers suggest that their heterosexual orientation provokes their interest in looking at the swimsuit issue. For example, when I asked one man why he likes the issue, he stated, "Because women are featured!" Another interviewed consumer comments that he enjoys the swimsuit issue because it represents "nice looking women," and that, "I don't know what's not to like about that, being a male."

Men who publicly declare that they are not attracted to or do not enjoy the swimsuit issue, even if they do not criticize the text, leave themselves open to questions about their heterosexual status. In fact, when heterosexual men articulate neutral or critical opinions of the swimsuit issue, they oftentimes announce their heterosexuality. An extreme example of this occurred when an interviewed consumer who heavily criticizes the swimsuit issue began his critique by stating, "I like women. I like all kinds of, all types of women. Women are beautiful to me." In a printed Letter to the Editor, another man complains about the lack of sports in the swimsuit issue, but while complaining he proclaims his heterosexuality and interest in women as sexual spectacle by saying, "I'm not weird or anything (I can see more on the covers of a least three other magazines I receive), but your priorities are a little mixed up" (February 11, 1974, p. 76).

The remarks of many female consumers imply that their heterosexual orientation causes their lack of interest in the swimsuit issue. For example, one interviewed woman, who has a neutral opinion of the swimsuit issue, says that she cannot even understand what men like about it, stating, "I'm not a man, so I don't know." Another interviewed woman consumer comments, "I guess it just wouldn't be something that I would be . . . interested in [enough to buy it] . . . My husband would probably buy it, but I wouldn't buy it." Sometimes female consumers are more explicit about the role their heterosexual orientation plays in shaping their views of the swimsuit issue. In 1974 *Sports Illustrated* printed a letter in which the woman writer asserts that, " . . . 'the sight of a pretty girl in a swimsuit against the backdrop of sun, sand and surf' doesn't do a thing for my 'midwinter blahs.' Do you plan a sequel featuring men in bikinis" (February 11, p. 76)? A woman whose letter appears in *Sports Illustrated* in 1989 writes, "Forget the girls in the swimsuits. Just send me a picture of Rick Reilly in his $28 Arrow shirt" (March 13, p. 10).

The assumption of natural, universal, and compelling heterosexuality even underlies the comments made by many people who articulate "liberal" critiques of the swimsuit issue. These consumers say that they object to the swimsuit issue because they think it discriminates against men of color and women. What they really mean is that the issue discriminates against heterosexual women and heterosexual men of color. When consumers argue that the underrepresentation of [women] models of color in the swimsuit issue discriminates against male consumers of color, they usually assume that men of color are all heterosexual. When consumers contend that *Sports Illustrated*'s practice of picturing only women models discriminates against women consumers, they usually assume that all women are heterosexual. In fact, many women who articulate liberal feminist critiques of the swimsuit issue base these critiques on their own heterosexual orientation. For example, an interviewed woman who views the swimsuit issue as sexist asserts, "When they start showing Joe Montana in a thong, . . . or something like that, to whet my appetite, fine, . . . then I'll sign up for twelve months." Other liberal feminist consumers assume that all women readers of *Sports Illustrated* are heterosexuals who wish to look at sexualized representations of men's bodies. For example, a woman's letter published in *Sports Illustrated* on February 28, 1983 says:

> Where are the men models? . . . I'm dying to see Jim Palmer in a sexy suggestive swimsuit. I've been reading *SI* for more than 10 years and I'm sure the percentage of women readers has climbed during that time. Don't we merit at least an insert? (p. 82)

Since most consumers think that the swimsuit issues feature sexualized representations of women, and that heterosexuality is natural, universal, and compelling, the knowledge that many women consume and enjoy the swimsuit issue may pose a problem. This problem prompts many consumers to believe that *if* women read the swimsuit issue, they must be appreciating the fashion and beauty ideals represented in the issue rather than viewing the models in a sexual way. In fact, women who wish to conform to normative definitions of heterosexuality may feel compelled to claim that they enjoy the fashion or role modeling if they read the issue, otherwise others may call their sexual identities into question. When consumers declare that men delight in the swimsuit issue for its display of sexuality, whereas women appreciate it for fashion or other non-sexual reasons, their statements rest upon the assumption of natural, universal, and compelling heterosexuality. As one interviewed consumer puts it, "If [the reader] was a man, I'd probably say it's attractive to them. They probably like looking at it. And then for a woman, it might be to see what's fashionable in swimwear." Another argued that men "would see it sexually," whereas women would see it as "'That's the way I want to be.'"

## Securing Heterosexual Status through Consumption

Since the meaning of the swimsuit issue is so closely tied to male heterosexuality, it is not surprising that many men consume the issue in public to affirm their heterosexual status. This corresponds with the tendency for people in corporate capitalist societies to seek to identify with a place in social structure by consuming certain objects, including media objects (e.g., Baudrillard, 1981; Smith, D. E., 1988; Williamson, 1985).

Some consumers appear to use discussion of the swimsuit issue as an opportunity to proclaim their own, or their relatives', conformity to heterosexual norms. In a Letter to the Editor, a woman writes that " . . . if my son gets to be 13 or 14 years old and doesn't look, I'll take him to a psychologist. If my husband stops looking, I'll know he is dead" (February 11, 1974, p. 76). I recruited three known gay male and two known lesbian consumers for this study, making them, in combination, thirteen percent of the interviewed consumers. Almost all of the other consumers implied during the interviews that they are heterosexual, although I did not actively pursue information about sexual orientation. For example, an interviewed consumer who enjoys the issue declared, "I like looking at chicks as much as the next guy."

Public affirmation of heterosexual status through the swimsuit issue goes beyond simple declarations of heterosexual identity. Some consumers pin pictures from the swimsuit issue on walls, share the issue with friends, and carry on extensive discussions about the issue with others. One interviewed consumer reports that his college roommate cut out pictures from the last three years of the swimsuit issue and put them on his dorm room walls, along with pictures of sports. Another interviewed consumer describes how he and his friends talk about the issue:

You just compare them, you know, what it would be like to go out with that girl or something . . . You just sit there and talk, you know, with . . . some of your buds, and go, "Oh man," you know, "I betcha she'd like me," or something. You just goof around and stuff . . . [My friends compare the models with] their girlfriends and like girls in the halls and on the streets and stuff. And, they'll like put [the models] as idols above everybody else, you know . . . like the all-star team, if you want to call it . . . You . . . like to look at 'em and just think about it and dream and wish and stuff.

Some boys/men go beyond simply talking about their attraction to the models. One interviewed model reports that "normal" "young guys" sent her mail that expresses how they are "seeing this beautiful woman and falling in love with her." Another interviewed model says she got "fan mail . . . from old men, young boys, and then men actually asking me out."

There is much societal pressure on boys/men to appear hetero-sexual, and since many people think that male attraction to sexual representations of women is a direct sign of heterosexual orientation, there is much pressure on males to publicly declare that they enjoy these representations. This pressure moves many boys/men to claim that they enjoy the swimsuit issue. One interviewed consumer discusses peer pressure among boys to appreciate the issue, and links this pres-sure to heterosexism:

A lot of [young male athletes] kind of go with the flow, you know, peer pressure . . . 'Cause, like, their friend'll open up the magazine and show them a girl and they'll say, "You don't like this girl? Oh, man, what's wrong with you? You should like this girl," and that kind of thing. And the kid might not even like girls, you know. So, it's like peer pressure . . . all around.

Much of the public discourse about, and many of the ways boys/men consume, the swimsuit issue reinforce the belief that nature com-pels male attraction to and enjoyment of sexual representations of women. This belief creates problems for both heterosexual and gay men. Heterosexual men who do not feel drawn toward or enjoy sexual representations of women may be moved to doubt their sexual orien-tation. While gay men who internalize the notions that they should be sexually attracted to women, and should enjoy consuming sexual rep-resentations of women, experience internalized homophobia.

Representations such as the swimsuit issue do not simply serve as vehicles to affirm heterosexuality—they help to legitimate the ideology of mandatory heterosexuality. Here, the term "mandatory heterosexual-ity" denotes the set of ideas that follows from the assumption that all people naturally are, or should be, heterosexual. Elements of social structure and culture that are rooted in this ideology oppress gay/ lesbian/bisexual people.

## Using Heterosexual Status to Secure Masculine Status

Heterosexuality is central to the manufacture of hegemonic masculinity (e.g., Carrigan, Connell & Lee, 1987; Connell, 1987; Herek, 1986). Connell (1987) even argues that "The most important feature of contemporary hegemonic masculinity is that it is heterosexual . . . " (p. 186). Connell (1987) introduced the concept of "hegemonic masculinity" to the academic world. In this book, hegemonic (or normative) masculinity refers to the dominant form of masculinity in United States society at the present time. Hegemonic masculinity tends to reflect and reinforce, rather than challenge, the present gender order. Thus, from a feminist perspective, many characteristics of hegemonic masculinity are problematic.

Men often work to publicly define themselves as heterosexual so that others will perceive them as masculine. When men publicly display an interest in sexual representations of women they can affirm not only their heterosexual status but also their masculine status (e.g., Dyer, R., 1985; Hite, 1981; Metcalf, 1985). Even possessing images of women who resemble the popular beauty ideal signifies masculinity to some degree (Freedman, 1986; Lakoff & Scherr, 1984). Pin-ups of women commonly appear in settings where boys/men predominate, settings where appearing masculine has its greatest impact. Men who do not experience attraction to or enjoyment of sexual representations of women may be impelled to doubt their masculinity. Men often use pin-ups of women to help them alleviate their insecurities about masculinity (Gabor, 1973; Hearn, 1985).

One reason that consumption of sexual representations of women enhances masculine status is because these representations often obsessively mark (perceived) physical differences between men and women. Many times it seems as if producers create these representations for the sole purpose of displaying physical gender difference. For example, producers often design these representations to accentuate breasts, a body part many people view as symbolic of women's physical difference from men. Thus, men can consume these representations to differentiate themselves from women (e.g., Finn, 1985; Kuhn, 1985; Peiss, 1989).

Earlier, I mentioned that many consumers view the swimsuit issue models as symbols of femininity, womanhood, or womens' difference from men. It appears that many consumers read the swimsuit issue as representing physical gender difference. The emphasis on gender difference in the swimsuit issue texts reinforces contemporary definitions of hegemonic femininity and masculinity.

There is plenty of evidence that consumption of the swimsuit issue is associated with masculinity. Although most consumers do not explicitly link the swimsuit issue to masculinity, as already illustrated, most hold that (mainly) men consume the swimsuit issue and other sexualized images of women. Linking men with consumption of the swimsuit issue helps to create the perception that there is an association between the swimsuit issue and masculinity.

Some consumers do explicitly connect consumption of the swimsuit issue, and other sexual representations, with masculinity. One interviewed consumer associates this consumption with a "men are macho" attitude, while another associates it with "virility":

> It's a virility issue, I think . . . Men who are couch potatoes or . . . arm chair coaches, they like to think of themselves as virile. And they like anything dealing with virility. And to see women in small bikinis, eenie-weenie, eenie-meanie-type bikinis would be tantalizing, I suppose, and go along with that virile image.

As already mentioned, through public consumption of the swimsuit issue, such as through the use of pin-ups or discussion with same-gender friends, boys/men mark themselves as heterosexual. Because heterosexuality is associated with masculinity, public consumption of the swimsuit issue also enhances masculine status. Of course, consumption of other texts that feature sexual representations of women can serve this purpose as well. But, the role pornography can play in securing heterosexual and masculine status is reduced by restrictions against its use in public settings. Thus, the number of boys/men who consume the swimsuit issue and other more "acceptable" forms of sexual representation is probably increased by prohibitions against pornography.

Many problems emanate from the fact that heterosexuality serves as a key component of the contemporary masculine ideal. It encourages heterosexual men to flaunt their heterosexuality to enhance their masculine status, while encouraging gay men to remain in the closet. Remaining in the closet creates many practical problems, and is quite unhealthy from a psychological perspective. Most significantly, when heterosexuality serves as a ticket to male legitimacy, heterosexual status itself becomes a badge of superiority, and this feeds the already rampant homophobia and heterosexism in United States society. In this climate, the oppression that gay/lesbian/bisexual people face goes way beyond irritating practical matters and psychological stress.

6

# Profiting from the Masculinity Crisis

In the last chapter, I argued that the swimsuit issue is about heterosexuality, that many boys/men mark themselves as heterosexual by consuming the issue in public, and that marking oneself as heterosexual through consuming the issue enhances one's masculine reputation. These arguments underlie the thesis layed out in this chapter, that *Sports Illustrated* is a magazine about hegemonic masculinity rather than a magazine about sport.

### The Masculinity Crisis[1] and Response to the Crisis

*Sports Illustrated* and its swimsuit issue must be seen in the context of contemporary gender relations. During the last few decades, the feminist movement struggled for and to some degree attained more power for women. These changes, and calls for more changes, in the gender order challenge hegemonic forms of masculinity (e.g., Dubbert, 1979; Kimmel, 1990; Messner, 1992). Some men respond with "support [for] feminist reforms" (p. 85), while others try to "restore a dominant masculinity," including "new cults of true masculinity" (Connell, 1995, p. 84). I think Paul Hoch (1979) was correct when he stated that in recent years, " . . . the quest of individual (or collective) manhood has eclipsed Christianity as an ontology for directing [men's] activity and orienting it toward a coherent, ultimate goal" (p. 15). Today, pressures for men to prove themselves as masculine are great. For many men, asserting masculinity has become "an almost existential struggle with nature (women being conceived of as the embodiment of nature), with other men, and with the limitations of his own biology" (Hoch, 1979, p. 16).

Thus, challenges to the gender order result in what some scholars have called masculine preserves. In this book, the term masculine preserve denotes an arena of social life that (many) men use to resist their (potential) loss of power. In recent years, these preserves have included the military, sport, sexuality, and interpersonal violence. Herek (1986) argues that recent changes in the gender order, and thus in masculinity, make heterosexuality even more central to normative definitions of masculinity. Thus, the extreme popularity of the swimsuit issue can be partly explained by changes in the gender order, as men who resist the changes increasingly depend on public declarations of heterosexual status to secure masculine status.

Mishkind, et al. (1986) have argued that one of the few remaining ways for men to express and preserve traditional masculinity may be through the literal embodiment of characteristics that are perceived as masculine. Note that all four of the examples of masculine preserves cited in the above paragraph are associated with physical gender difference. Men use these preserves to claim that their bodies are vastly different from the bodies of women. In recent years, discourse that highlights physical gender difference, that reflects and reinforces the belief that men's and women's bodies are naturally dichotomous, has served as the main ideological foundation for men's dominance (e.g., Bartky, 1988; Horowitz & Kaufman, 1987; Woodhouse, 1989).

In the last chapter, I discussed the important part heterosexuality and male consumption of sexual representations of women play in current definitions of hegemonic masculinity. In the rest of this section, I focus on how sport, and male consumption of representations of sport, also play a central role in defining hegemonic masculinity.

Some scholars argue that sport serves as a masculine preserve (e.g., Hargreaves, 1986; Sheard & Dunning, 1973; Willis, 1982). Men use sport and representations of sport to mark men's bodies as strong, agile, powerful, and active, traits commonly associated with hegemonic masculinity (e.g., Connell, 1987; Dyer, R., 1982; Gagnon, 1976; Messner, 1988). Sport serves an important role in securing consent for the present gender order because people use it to manufacture and reinforce beliefs in physical gender dichotomization (Hargreaves, 1986; Willis, 1982).

Media coverage of sport often features masculinity as a central theme (e.g., Ford, 1982; Green & Jenkins, 1982; Hollands, 1984), and thus reinforces the use of sport as a masculine preserve. Women in sport receive little media coverage. When women athletes do get coverage, a variety of forms of gender bias often appears.[2] Duncan (1990) contends that sport media texts often suggest a male ideal subject position.

Some scholars argue that males use sport spectatorship to enhance their masculine reputations and experience solidarity with other men. As Fasteau (1980) explains:

In most spectator sports, especially football, qualities thought to be masculine are at a premium. Men understand and identify with these values and codes even if they are not athletes themselves. By devoted spectating and rooting, they vicariously affirm their membership in the club of certified males. (pp. 48–49)

Solidarity among men seems especially evident when the sport involves contact, partly explaining the popularity of media coverage of contact sports with male consumers (e.g., Fasteau, 1980; Gagnon, 1976; Messner, 1987). Many male consumers like representations of men with large muscles, as the muscles signify strength, power, activity, and masculinity (Dyer, R., 1982; Gagnon, 1976; Messner, 1988; Mishkind, Rodin, Silberstein & Streigel-Moore, 1986). Chorbajian (1978) observes that we even associate media derived knowledge about sport with masculinity.

Advertisers value the dominant form of sport coverage in the United States because the audience it attracts features a high percentage of relatively affluent adult men. Advertisers view this type of audience as hard-to-reach but lucrative, so media producers can charge advertisers high rates for advertising around sports coverage (Coakley, 1986; Greendorfer, 1983; Leiss, Kline & Jhally, 1986).

Eitzen and Sage (1982) argue that there are a number of reasons why mostly men consume mediated sport: many people see sport as a masculine preserve, girl/women athletes receive less coverage, people often discourage girls/women from consuming mediated sport, and girls/women develop less interest in mediated sport due to more limited opportunities for participation in competitive sport (Eitzen & Sage, 1982). G. Dyer (1987) explains how the mass media works to discourage women from mediated sport involvement:

Men are clearly targeted by the scheduling of television sports in their leisure time (i.e. at weekends) and, by and large, women are regarded as outsiders or a third party in the "genre's" mode of address. They are involved neither in the rules/science of the game nor in the celebration of male values and physique. (p. 8)

Producers of sports coverage seek a male audience, and then the predominantly male audience that most sport coverage draws perpetuates the use of sport as a masculine preserve. One wonders to what degree these media practices are driven by sexism, and to what degree they are driven by the pursuit of profit.

## *Fashioning* Sports Illustrated *as a Men's Magazine*

Private media operate as businesses, with the central goal being profit. In order to understand *Sports Illustrated*, one must view the magazine as a business. One needs to understand what business strategies *Sports Illustrated* producers use, why they employ these strategies, how they implement these strategies, and whether these strategies work.

### *Motive for the Strategy*

Most of the interviewed producers describe profit as the primary motive for the production of *Sports Illustrated* and the swimsuit issue. As one interviewed producer comments, "Every issue of the magazine is a revenue producing issue of the magazine. That's why we do fifty-two of them each year." Another remarks, "It's all about sales, selling magazines. That's publishing, in the bottom line. Publishing is about selling magazines."

Today, advertising is the largest source of revenue for mass circulation magazines, and this economic situation greatly influences magazine content. This situation reduces the direct influence of consumers, while amplifying the influence of advertisers (e.g., Murdock, 1982; Turow, 1984; Wilson, C. C. & Gutierrez, 1985). An illustration of this is that in the early 1990s the editors of *Ms* magazine stopped including advertisements, because they felt that advertisers wielded too much influence on the magazine content (Steinem, 1990).

Publishers regard magazines not so much as products to sell to readers, but as vehicles to sell target audience groups to advertisers. For producers, particular audience groups, rather than magazines, have become the product. Publishers who can generate a large audience that contains a high percentage of consumers from a desirable category can charge advertisers more money (e.g., Freund, 1980; Leiss, Kline & Jhally, 1986; Wilson, C. C. & Gutierrez, 1985).

In fashioning magazines to draw particular categories of consumers, publishers tend to reinforce traditional social distinctions (e.g., Leiss, Kline & Jhally, 1986; Peterson, 1964; Wilson, C. C. & Gutierrez, 1985). Early in the history of magazine production, publishers developed magazines focused on being a woman to attract a general audience of women (Ferguson, 1983; Fishburn, 1982). According to some scholars, magazines for men tend to address specific themes or elements of life, not the more general theme of being a man. Standard themes of men's magazines include crime, war, hunting, sports, speed, and sex (Ferguson, 1983; Peterson, 1964).

The product produced by *Sports Illustrated* is not the magazine itself, but is a large audience of relatively affluent male consumers. Although sports coverage itself often draws a considerable audience of men, I believe that producers pursue additional profits by fashioning *Sports Illustrated* to beckon an audience that goes beyond the men who actively participate in sport. I think that it is to this end that producers structure the magazine content around the theme of hegemonic masculinity. That is, producers create content that suggests that *Sports Illustrated* is a "men's magazine," rather than simply a "sports magazine."

## Description of the Strategy

By presenting content that features the combination of elite men's spectator sports and sexualized images of women, the producers develop an image of *Sports Illustrated* that many associate with hegemonic masculinity. Although both of these themes signify masculinity by themselves, when they appear together they create an even stronger emphasis on hegemonic masculinity.

In *Sports Illustrated,* the celebration of men athletic heroes, who serve as symbols of hegemonic masculine values such as physical strength, competitiveness, success, active agency, aggression/violence, and power, contributes to the creation of the tone of hegemonic masculinity that pervades the magazine. The fact that the magazine mainly covers men's professional sport and elite amateur sport (e.g., the winners in Division I men's college sport) accentuates characteristics associated with hegemonic masculinity. The types of sports covered also highlight these characteristics. For example, football and boxing showcase the characteristics of strength, aggression, and violence. Male athletes who participate in sports which do not emphasize these characteristics, such as bowling and figure skating, receive much less coverage.

Sometimes *Sports Illustrated* texts contain representations of sport that suggest meanings about gender that differ from the usual emphasis on hegemonic masculinity, and thus seem to challenge the sport-masculinity connection, such as coverage of women's sport and men's sports that are not associated with masculinity. Women athletes' demonstration of strength, competitiveness, aggression, and power, as well as men athletes' demonstration of grace, can call into question the idea of natural physical gender dichotomization and thus endanger the use of sport as a masculine preserve. Yet, scholars argue that *Sports Illustrated* minimizes the opposition that women athletes represent by containing only tokenistic coverage of women athletes; by focusing on women's sports and women athletes who do not represent strong challenges to gender norms; by structuring the coverage of women's sport so that it focuses on hegemonic gender meanings; and by featuring representations of women in advertisements, stories about men's sport, and the swimsuit issue that reaffirm hegemonic gender meanings (Boutilier & SanGiovanni, 1983; Duncan, 1990; 1993; Hanna, 1983; Kane, 1988; Lumpkin & Williams, 1989; Reid & Soley, 1979; Williams, L., & Lumpkin, 1989).[3]

It is possible that *Sports Illustrated* has discovered the most profitable way to cover sport. Because the coverage of women's sport and men's sports that are not associated with masculinity remains at a tokenistic level, and is usually presented in ways that do little to challenge the sports-masculinity bond, it does not disturb the reader who is attracted to the hegemonic masculine tone of the magazine. On the other hand, the tokenistic coverage may help *Sports Illustrated* secure further profits from consumers who follow women's and "secondary" men's sports or do not identify with the tone of hegemonic masculinity. The fact that few other media texts feature quality coverage of these sports make *Sports Illustrated* one of the few sources to look to for this coverage.

As already mentioned, the swimsuit issue also helps to create the perception that there is an association between hegemonic masculinity and *Sports Illustrated* because the issue involves the representation of women as aesthetic and sexual spectacle for men, thus defining the entire *Sports Illustrated* male readership as unquestioningly heterosexual. Some of the sports coverage and advertisements in *Sports Illustrated* also perform this function, as women athletes, women in advertisements, and women connected to men's sporting events are often represented as sexual spectacle for men (Davis, L. R., 1993; Duncan, 1990; 1993; Kane, 1988). Through this type of coverage, *Sports Illustrated* beckons heterosexual male consumers (Davis, L. R., 1993).

The perceptual link producers of *Sports Illustrated* create between the magazine and male heterosexual status discourages present and future consumption by gay men, lesbians, bisexuals, and heterosexual women. In fact, the content of *Sports Illustrated* works to conceal the existence of, and thus delegitimate, the lives of gay men and lesbians. The delegitimation of gay/lesbian lives reinforces the rampant heterosexism in United States society.

The swimsuit issue draws the attention of a wider group of men to *Sports Illustrated* by helping to define the content of the magazine not simply as "sport coverage" but as "hegemonic masculine culture," which includes a focus on both sport and mandatory heterosexuality.

Thus, although the swimsuit issue generates considerable profit all by itself, I believe that producers also use it as a tool to increase the number of male consumers who purchase other issues of the magazine.

There is another reason why *Sports Illustrated* might announce the heterosexuality of its readership so loudly. Sport may not be able to serve the function of masculine preserve as well as scholars have previously assumed, because some of the ways men practice sporting activities signify homosexuality and thus lack of masculinity. Sport participation is one of the few social arenas in United States society where men are allowed to touch other men. Men usually participate in and watch sport in a homosocial environment, with other men. Male sport spectators look at, scrutinize, appreciate, and even worship the bodies of other men (Messner, 1992; Morse, 1983; Pronger, 1990). Thus, a strong declaration of heterosexual status by *Sports Illustrated* may be necessary to ward off any homosexual/feminine connotations that men's sporting practices convey.

Interestingly, only a few other scholars have discussed the fact that the themes of men's sport and heterosexuality are often articulated in the same arena (Connell, 1990; Fine, 1987; Pronger, 1990; Trujillo, 1991). This is despite the fact that in coverage of men's sporting events, women often appear as aesthetic/sexual display (Davis, L. R., 1993; 1994; Duncan, 1990; 1993; McKay & Rowe, 1987).

*Producers' Role in the Strategy*

For the most part, I do not think that *Sports Illustrated* producers consciously pursue content that reflects the theme of hegemonic masculinity. Instead, I think that their strategies emanate from the pursuit of profit. In their endeavor to secure the greatest possible profits, they attempt to attract the largest possible audience of (affluent) male consumers. Since men are quite different from each other, the producers probably (subconsciously) use the dominant ideal of masculinity as their guide, following the path of "least resistance" by avoiding most topics that deviate from hegemonic masculine norms and emphasizing topics that exemplify these norms.

The interviewed advertising employee claims that the producers do not shape *Sports Illustrated* to reach particular people. Nevertheless, information obtained from the marketing and sales department at *Sports Illustrated* implies that the magazine targets affluent men. The gender and income of the consumers of the magazine are highlighted in brochures and such that the magazine uses to attract advertisers. For example, one publication *Sports Illustrated* distributes to advertisers compares *Sports Illustrated* to other magazines that men commonly read (Simmons Market Research Bureau, 1991).

Although none of the interviewed producers directly stated that the swimsuit issue and sports coverage reflect the theme of hegemonic masculinity, some maintain that the swimsuit spread "just seems to fit" into *Sports Illustrated*. Explanations for this general sense of connection usually remain unarticulated, but a couple of the interviewed producers point out that the magazine readers appreciate the swimsuit spread, and that the spread fits into "the culture" of the magazine. In commenting about the swimsuit issue, one interviewed producer explains, "I don't really think there's any relation to the magazine, except that it's part of the culture of the magazine to do it now." The only interviewed producer to voice criticism of the swimsuit issue makes a more explicit connection between the readers of the magazine, their "culture," and the swimsuit issue by considering the gender of the readers:

> The only connection that I can clearly see is the fact that there are a lot of sportsmen, who are into sports, who are also into pin-up magazines, girlie magazines, sexual magazines and that kind of material . . . [And], clearly [the swimsuit issue and] those types of items appear within all male or predominately male environments.

Although some interviewed producers deny that *Sports Illustrated* specifically markets particular issues of the magazine, producers do use the swimsuit issue to promote and attract more subscribers to *Sports Illustrated*. Other producers state that *Sports Illustrated* uses all of the special issues, including the swimsuit issue, to sell subscriptions to the magazine.

*Sports Illustrated* markets to potential subscribers through direct mail, magazine insert cards, and direct response television advertisements. The direct mail campaigns use mailing lists which feature people who live within certain zip codes, have subscribed to the magazine in the past, read magazines, like sports, are men, and fit within particular age and income brackets. The swimsuit issue commonly appears in advertisements for *Sports Illustrated,* demonstrating that the producers are using the swimsuit issue as a drawing card to get readers to subscribe or renew subscriptions. These advertisements also provide evidence that the magazine's producers view the swimsuit issue as an integral part of the magazine.

According to one interviewed producer, another way producers use the swimsuit issue to market *Sports Illustrated* is by hiring the cover model to work on public relations campaigns for the magazine. This producer says that the most popular *Sports Illustrated* public relations events feature the swimsuit issue models. The cover model accompanies the advertising sales director and creative director to sales offices across the country. These offices sponsor luncheons where advertising clients, and other organizations or individuals with which *Sports Illustrated* conducts business, meet the model and hear about the production of the swimsuit issue. *Sports Illustrated* also sponsors cocktail parties that the swimsuit issue models attend or that feature these models. The producers host a big promotional party in New York when the swimsuit issue comes out.

The public relations employees at *Sports Illustrated* feed other media organizations information about the magazine, including stories about the swimsuit issue. If the cover model (along with other *Sports Illustrated* employees) goes to a particular area, the public relations employees often contact the local television stations to secure coverage of the visit. According to one interviewed producer, because of the controversy surrounding the swimsuit issue, the public relations employees carefully monitor the process of distributing information related to the swimsuit issue. In recent years, prior to the release of the swimsuit issue each winter, some news media have covered the issue. The coverage is usually very positive and features pictures of the models. This suggests that the public relations employees at *Sports Illustrated* play a major role in securing the news coverage.

## Success of the Strategy

Earlier sections of this book have demonstrated that regardless of producers' conscious intentions, consumers view *Sports Illustrated* as a men's magazine and associate its content with masculinity. Eight of the interviewed consumers imply that the combination of sports coverage and the swimsuit issue help to create the masculine image of *Sports Illustrated*. Two interviewed consumers straightforwardly state that both the swimsuit issue and sports are associated with masculinity. As one puts it, both "cater to some kind of macho image which is very prevalent in society." Other consumers do not explicitly discuss masculinity but hold that it is mainly men who consume both sport and the swimsuit issue or other sexualized images of women. For example, an interviewed consumer who thinks that the swimsuit issue resembles pornography explains that the producers "know that predominately males get the magazine, for the sports, and that males are going to, of course, be attracted [to the swimsuit issue]." A couple of the interviewed consumers argue that producers publish the swimsuit spread in the context of sports coverage because boys/men often have fantasies about both sports and relationships with women. These consumers feel that the content of *Sports Illustrated* appeals to boys/men because boys/men often fantasize that sport involvement or achievement will enable them to meet "the girl" in the swimsuit issue or procure relationships with desirable women. One of these consumers argues that "the armchair quarterback" thinks:

> "Well, if I was there [as a superstar athlete], I could have it all . . . I could have money. I could have women. I could have whatever" . . . And so, . . . the sex plus the sports . . . Sex sells, and if you can put sex with something else that is popular and that sells well, which happens to be sports, [you will sell even more].

Efforts to draw men by creating a tone of hegemonic masculinity works: most of the consumers of *Sports Illustrated* are men, and many of these men are affluent. In a 1988 study of national edition subscribers (Don Bowden Associates, 1988), the researchers report that the subscribers are 90.9 percent male, with a median household income of $51,389 and a mean household income of $63,745. Another study (Simmons Market Research Bureau, 1991) compares *Sports Illustrated* to other popular magazines that men commonly read, and finds that *Sports Illustrated* attracts a higher percentage of men readers than general news magazines, business magazines, and even *Gentlemen's Quarterly* and *Esquire*. Only *Playboy* draws a higher percentage of men readers.

The fact that *Sports Illustrated* is one of the most popular magazines in the United States[4] (*Advertising Age,* 1990; Greendorfer, 1983) means that a large percentage of the male population in the United States reads the magazine. One study (Simmons Market Research Bureau, 1991) indicates that the magazine reaches 19.8 percent of men over eighteen years of age, and 21.8 percent of men that make over $25,000, in the United States.

I suspect that a significant number of these consumers are using *Sports Illustrated* as "cultural capital." According to O'Sullivan et al. (1994), cultural capital denotes "symbolic power" that is derived from "unequal distribution of cultural practices, values and competences characteristic of capitalist societies" (p. 73). Producers of media texts make available potential identities to the consumer by creating images for their texts. A desire to associate with these identities sometimes moves the consumer to purchase these texts (e.g., Barthel, 1988; Graham, 1987; Williamson, 1985). Consumers can possess magazines, and thus often use magazine consumption to express particular self images and group affiliations (Meyrowitz, 1985). Men who learn to value hegemonic masculinity can, to some degree, symbolically affirm their conformity to masculine norms by consuming *Sports Illustrated* in the presence of others.

During adolescence, a time when girls and boys often meet intense pressure to conform to societal expectations regarding gender and sexuality, people commonly expect boys to publicly display an interest in and knowledge of men's sports and a sexual interest in girls/women. Consumption of *Sports Illustrated* can help relieve such pressures.

Recent challenges to and changes in the gender order, which have stimulated the current masculinity crisis and the backlash against the challenges and changes, increase the popularity of texts like *Sports Illustrated*. Sports and sexuality are two of the few remaining strongholds of masculinity. As many men struggle to maintain gender-related forms of privilege, they utilize elite men's spectator sports and heterosexual relations to define their difference from women. Because *Sports Illustrated* highlights these two themes, males can experience pleasure from consumption of the magazine, as such consumption reinforces definitions of themselves as different from and superior to women. Thus, affirmation of hegemonic masculine status through consumption of *Sports Illustrated* is not a politically neutral activity.

Although many men use *Sports Illustrated*, *Sports Illustrated* also uses these men, capitalizing on their desires and insecurities. I believe that *Sports Illustrated* reaps considerable profit from advertisers because the tone of hegemonic masculinity that pervades the magazine draws a large number of relatively affluent men consumers. I do not think it is a coincidence that in the mid-1960s, when the swimsuit issue officially began, *Sports Illustrated* texts started to beckon solely men viewers, started to place a greater emphasis on spectator sports that we commonly associate with masculinity, and first began to produce a profit.

Today, compared to other magazines in the United States, *Sports Illustrated* receives one of the highest amounts of advertising revenue (Erickson, 1987; Kang, 1988), with over $247 million in advertising revenue reported in 1986 (Erickson, 1987). In particular, *Sports Illustrated* reports much higher figures for advertising revenue than other sports magazines (*Advertising Age*, 1990; Erickson, 1987).

### Critiques of the Sports Illustrated Strategy

Although the tone of hegemonic masculinity that pervades *Sports Illustrated* results in enormous profits for the producers, and may be appreciated by those who worship the hegemonic masculine ideal, not everyone approves of *Sports Illustrated*'s tactics. Criticisms of the swim-suit issue that reflect the consumers' disapproval of the hegemonic masculine ideal itself will be discussed in the next chapter. Here, I focus only on consumer criticisms of the way *Sports Illustrated* uses this ideal.

### The Issue Is a Sensationalized Sales Gimmick

Some consumers seem to sense that the swimsuit issue is being used to increase subscriptions to *Sports Illustrated,* and voice disapproval of this practice. Thus, a few interviewed consumers disapprove of the swimsuit issue because they view it as a sensationalized sales gimmick. For example, one interviewed consumer, who enjoys looking at the swimsuit spread, says:

> You don't need to do this. You sell your magazine, you do very good coverage of sports, [so] why do you have to sensationalize? . . . And, to me . . . it's just basically a sales gimmick . . . And, I hap-pen to frown upon that . . . Originally, it was a nice touch. Then it got to be a little too much, just for the sake of selling the magazine.

Another interviewed consumer comments, "It's a marketing ploy . . . I don't think a magazine with that kind of [good] reputation needs to stoop to that kind of stuff."

The fact that producers often use the swimsuit issue to market *Sports Illustrated* magazine, such as featuring the swimsuit issue in television advertisements for the magazine, may encourage consumers to create this reading. But, to read the issue in this manner, consumers need to employ a perspective that involves at least some criticism of advertising and/or other elements of contemporary capitalist marketing.

If consumers perceived the swimsuit spread as expressing sport-related meaning, then they would see the spread as part of the normal sports coverage. So, it is clear that consumers who view the swimsuit issue as a sales gimmick do not see the issue as expressing any significant sport-related meaning.

About half of the interviewed consumers hold that there is abso-lutely no relationship between sports and the swimsuit issue. For ex-ample, one interviewed consumer asserted that the swimsuit issue does not have "a damn thing" to do with sport. Most of the other half of the interviewed consumers believe that the issue has a slight relationship to sport. These consumers mention two connections between the swimsuit issue and sport: that the representation of swimsuits links the issue to the sport of swimming, and that the producers select athletic and/or fit models.

In this regard, the intentions of the producers match consumer interpretations. Although the interviewed producers do not see sport as central to the meaning they try to express in the swimsuit issue, they do claim that they select athletic or fit models and perceive connections between the swimsuit issue and the sport of swimming. One interviewed producer remarks:

> We're a sports magazine, so the [swimsuit issue] pictures are supposed to show a kind of a sporting attitude toward the appreciation and enjoyment of swimming at the beach and wearing swim clothes . . . Swimming and swimwear are definitely part of our domain.

Another interviewed producer notes that producers select "very athletic-seeming" models. Of course, the models are not athletes, and *Sports Illustrated* fails to cover the sport of swimming in any depth during the rest of the year.

Several factors encourage consumers to perceive some connection between sport and the swimsuit issue. The fact that the issue appears in a magazine ostensibly devoted to covering sport, and the fact that many people define swimming as a sport, may encourage some consumers to connect the swimsuit issue to sport. Sometimes the written texts and poses in the swimsuit issue suggest athletic activity. For example, the captions commonly refer to the model's fitness (e.g., 1982; 1987; 1989) or athletic ability (e.g., 1970; 1985; 1987), and to athletic activities such as stretching (1973). Slender models appear in the issues, and many consumers associate thinness with physical fitness.

There are also many factors that exhort consumers to dismiss any connections between sport and the swimsuit issue. Elements of the swimsuit spread that resemble the genres of pornography or fashion advertisement encourage consumers to define the issue as outside the genre of sports coverage. The fact that the pictures do not show models with (much) muscle definition or competing in sport contributes to this view. When the models pose in "athletic" ways, the positioning often looks incorrect and immature. Readily available knowledge regarding the type of swimwear most women wear when they swim discourages the interpretation that the swimsuit issue expresses sport-related meaning, because this type of swimwear rarely appears in the swimsuit issue. As one interviewed consumer articulates it, "The swimsuits they show aren't going to be used in any athletic type [activity] . . . They're revealing." Consumers also know that swimsuit issue producers picture fashion models rather than athletes.

Sports Illustrated *Should Be about Sport*

Some consumers criticize the swimsuit spread because they say that it does not represent sport coverage and thus should not appear in *Sports Illustrated* magazine. Thirty-eight percent of the interviewed consumers articulated this view. As one declares:

> *Sports Illustrated* is a magazine that has an agenda. It talks about sports and athletes. And for just one month of the year, it's just pure junk. I mean, all it is, is half-naked women in swimming suits . . . They're not athletes that they're interviewing. It's not like the magazine is full of women swimmers. I mean, it is nothing to do with what they do for the other eleven months of the year . . . If that's the one month of the year that there are no sports going on, then there are plenty of people to interview or talk [to]. I mean, there are other subjects they could do for that month . . . People are interested in sports. They want to see interviews with athletes, they want to know what's going on in the sports world.

Similarly, in a letter from the February 10, 1975 issue of *Sports Illustrated*, a writer exclaims, "*SI* should concern itself with the latest sports events. Pin-ups I can get in a girlie magazine" (p. 66).

To create this reading, consumers must go beyond the belief that the swimsuit issue does not express sport-related meaning, because some consumers who hold this belief do not disapprove of the presence of the spread in *Sports Illustrated*. To generate this reading, consumers must believe that *Sports Illustrated* should cover only sports.

Those who create this reading take part in a debate over what should count as appropriate content in *Sports Illustrated*. Specifically, this struggle is over whether *Sports Illustrated* should cover solely sports or should cover topics that go beyond sports (i.e., non-sport topics that signify hegemonic masculinity). When consumers create this reading, they are rejecting the notion that *Sports Illustrated* should be a more general "men's magazine." *Sports Illustrated's* own narrow definition of sport, which producers articulate through the heavy coverage of elite men's spectator sport in the magazine, may actually encourage readers to reject the swimsuit issue, as the swimsuit spread clearly does not fit this narrow definition. On the other hand, if people view *Sports Illustrated* as a "men's magazine," rather than as a sports magazine, then the context of the magazine may actually encourage readers to see the swimsuit spread as appropriate content for the magazine.

Sports Illustrated *Should Be for Women, Too*

Consumers who think that *Sports Illustrated* inappropriately ignores women are engaged in a slightly different debate. This debate is over which athletes *Sports Illustrated* should cover, and which readers *Sports Illustrated* should address. One side contends that *Sports Illustrated* should provide equal coverage of male and female athletes, while the other side holds that (considerably) more coverage should be devoted to male athletes. One side explicitly argues that the (significant) audience for *Sports Illustrated* is, or should be, both men and women, whereas the other side more indirectly implies that the (significant) audience is, or should be, just men.

Some consumers claim that *Sports Illustrated* is sexist because it does not treat [heterosexual] women consumers in the same manner as [heterosexual] men consumers. These consumers maintain that when producers picture only women models in the swimsuit issue they provide [heterosexual] men consumers with sexual representation that they enjoy while neglecting to offer [heterosexual] women consumers the same form of enjoyment. Thus, they challenge *Sports Illustrated* to acknowledge [heterosexual] women readers. As already mentioned, those who create this reading often make the assumption that heterosexuality is universal, ignoring the interests of gay men, lesbians, and bisexuals. One interviewed woman consumer declares that when *Sports Illustrated* "show[s] equality across the board" by showing men in "skimpy little suits" then she "won't have a gripe." Several interviewed consumers argue that this type of sexism stems from "the sexual double standard" that pervades United States society. One interviewed consumer describes this double standard:

> The [male] teenager that scores with the woman is coming into his manhood and he's just wonderful. And a woman or a girl that has intercourse is just considered, you know, a tramp . . . You don't see *Good Housekeeping* have a men's swimsuit issue.

In fact, the media features endless images that highlight women's bodies, while featuring far fewer images that highlight men's bodies in a similar manner. Media producers often take men's bodies for granted and exempt them from the type of scrutiny and exposure women's bodies endure. The right to visually survey other people is a form of power, whereas being the object of this type of surveillance is associated with a lack of power. Thus, many men find it threatening to be viewed as aesthetic objects and resist such uses of men's bodies. In particular, many men view male homosexuality as very intimidating because they associate it with the lack of power that comes from being an object of visual surveillance and sexual appropriation (Coward, 1985; Reynaud, 1983).

Some consumers also accuse *Sports Illustrated* producers of sexism because they fail to represent women athletes in an equitable manner, and many link this accusation to criticism of the swimsuit issue. For example, one interviewed consumer emphatically argues:

> *Sports Illustrated* magazine, instead of having a spread of Martina in there, because she's a top sportswoman and a top money-maker, instead you get some little twenty-two year old bubble-head who's shagging her ass around. So, let's show the champions in *Sports Illustrated* where women are concerned, too, and let the rest of it go to *Penthouse* or into *Elle* or into *Cosmopolitan* where this kind of crap belongs . . . The focus on women in that magazine is for their bare asses. It's not on their leadership, on how much money they make in sports every year, how women excel in sports. No! It's the same old business, tits and ass . . . To me, that's what their signal is. It's just that loud and blunt to me . . . They're featuring top athletes in *Sports Illustrated*, but they're all men. And women are relegated to doing the nudey pages.

One letter writer links a critique of *Sports Illustrated*'s gender-biased sport coverage with the lack of male models in the swimsuit issue:

> The portrayal of sexuality per se is not offensive . . . What is offensive is that only this aspect of women is shown, while their legitimate role in sport is ignored. Meanwhile, men's role in sport is well reported while their sensuality, interestingly enough, is never mentioned. (February 12, 1973, p.78)

Several factors inspire consumers to believe that *Sports Illustrated* inappropriately ignores women. Obviously, the fact that the swimsuit issue texts (for the most part) feature exclusively women models, and the fact that *Sports Illustrated* only covers women athletes in a tokenistic manner, provide a crucial foundation for this reading. To a small degree, producers encourage consumers to create this reading when they feature this point of view in written text. Twice in the 1980s the editors even responded to the requests by women letter writers who wanted to see pictures of sexy men by printing pictures of male athletes in the Letters to the Editor section.[5] Of course, this gesture does not come close to the equality that these liberal feminist consumers demand.

To advance the notion that *Sports Illustrated* and its swimsuit issue should be for [heterosexual] women as well as [heterosexual] men, the consumer must employ a liberal feminist perspective. Liberal feminist discourse has become much more common in recent years in the United States, and correspondingly, increasing numbers of consumers articulate a liberal feminist reading of the swimsuit issue. As an interviewed producer observes, "Some women have started saying, 'Why don't you use men in the swimsuit issue? I'd like to see men,' which is kind of a new comment the last couple of years."

Some feminist consumers limit their critique of *Sports Illustrated* to demands that the magazine fully recognize women athletes and [heterosexual] women consumers. Other feminists go beyond these demands to condemn the sexism that underlies the unequal representation of men and women. This leads them to denounce the ideals of hegemonic masculinity and femininity themselves. The debate over these gender ideals is the focus of the chapter that follows.

# The Struggle over Gender

Because the central meaning of *Sports Illustrated* and its swimsuit issue is rooted in the ideal of hegemonic masculinity, it is logical that these texts serve as catalysts for debating issues of gender. Whether one holds reactionary, conservative, liberal, or radical ideas about the current gender order influences the position one takes in the debate.

## *Men Who Identify with Hegemonic Masculinity*

Men who hold conservative ideas about the gender order often wish to be associated with hegemonic masculinity, as this form of masculinity serves the current (and to some degree, past) gender order. As previously mentioned, these men often work to create public images of themselves as sporting virile heterosexuals, and thus *Sports Illustrated* and the swimsuit issue can serve as a tool for the manufacture of this image. Men who work to create this image often claim that they enjoy the swimsuit issue because they are naturally attracted to its display of "ideally beautiful and sexy women."

Many men, including thirty-three percent of the interviewed consumers, indicate that they enjoy the swimsuit issue because they appreciate the ideal femininity, beauty, and sexiness of the models. For example, one interviewed consumer remarks, "What's not to like? . . . A beautiful girl, . . . that's the aspect of it I like." Another interviewed consumer maintains that he used to like the swimsuit issue because the models served as "sexual fantasies" that "excited" him, noting that "You could stare at this in your bedroom and stuff . . . It was like, 'Oh wow! Look at her, you can see her chest! Oooh.' " In 1984 one writer, whose letter appears in *Sports Illustrated*, thanks the publishers for presenting "six gorgeous paragons of femininity" (February 27, p. 82). Some men even express romantic longings to meet or marry the models, as in 1977 when one man queries, "Paulina Porizkova, will you marry me?" (February 24, p. 77). In 1986 *Sports Illustrated* printed a letter from a man who requests the address and telephone number of a model.

This is the reading of the swimsuit issue that producers hope their male readers will make. One interviewed producer says that *Sports Illustrated* puts "the hottest girls . . . in there," so that men enjoy the issue. Producers regularly encourage this reading by repetitively representing it in written text. For example, in the 1989 25th anniversary swimsuit issue in an article about the history of the issue, the author says that many men like the swimsuit issues more than pornography. Producers constantly print letters from men that express adulation of the models for their (perceived) beauty or sexiness. Sometimes *Sports Illustrated* producers present information or pictures that compliment the reactions of these consumers in the Letters to the Editor section. Since the late 1970s, the editors commonly respond to readers in the Letter to the Editor section by printing pictures of particular models that male letter writers request.[1] In 1964 and 1979,[2] the editor responded to requests by providing information about whether the models were "taken" by other men. Although titles above the Letters to the Editor section can often be interpreted in multiple ways, at least one of these ways usually affirms consumers who appreciate the beauty and sexuality of the models. For example, consumers can interpret the title "Paradisiacal Revelations" (January 26, 1970) as expressing enjoyment of bodies that have been revealed, and the title "Sunstruck" (January 30, 1972) as indicating infatuation with the models.

*Sports Illustrated* reinforces the current form of gender inequality by creating a text that caters to a conservative response to the contemporary masculinity crisis. *Sports Illustrated* also helps to legitimate gender inequality by affirming a form of femininity that is consonant with this conservative masculine ideal.

### Women Who Identify with Hegemonic Femininity

Women who hold conservative views about the gender order usually do not articulate liberal, radical, or reactionary critiques of the swimsuit issue. In other words, they do not create the reactionary reading that the swimsuit issue is improper because sexual representation is immoral. They also do not express any feminist criticisms of the swimsuit issue. These women usually produce one of two readings: either holding that they have a neutral opinion of the swimsuit issue, or saying that they appreciate the issue for its display of fashion and/or role models.

Four of the interviewed female consumers (twenty-one percent of the women) say that they possess a neutral opinion of the swimsuit issue. Women who articulate this opinion state that they lack interest in the swimsuit issue, and yet do not object to it. One interviewed woman consumer comments, "I don't have any feeling [about the swimsuit issue] one way or the other . . . I don't necessarily like it or dislike it . . . I wouldn't ban it. I wouldn't protest because of what's in the issue." Another re-marked, "I have no interest in it," and "It just is not appealing to me."

For women who support the current gender order, this is the easiest reading of the swimsuit issue to create. When women read the issue as representing fashion and/or role models for them, they need to ignore, downplay, or reject a significant component of the common denotative meaning: that the issue is sexual display for men. On the other hand, women who articulate a neutral reading of the swimsuit issue do not need to reject this denotative level meaning. In fact, believing that the issue consists of sexual display for men probably compels many women who are faithful to the hegemonic feminine ideal to create a neutral reading.

Women who vocalize neutral readings of the swimsuit issue want no part in the debate over gender. They want to leave the social meaning of sexual representations of women completely up to others. Yet, by adopting a neutral position, they tacitly participate in the gender debate. Their remarks imply that women are so different from men that women cannot possibly understand men and have no business commenting on masculinity. A commitment to hegemonic femininity underlies this sub-mission to an absolute sense of gender difference. Women who create neutral readings do not critique hegemonic femininity, leaving societal definitions of femininity up to others. They tacitly indicate approval of the use of sport and sexual representations of women as masculine preserves. Their silence signals complicity in the hegemonic masculine project, and thus in the current gender order as well.

Most feminist media scholars do not acknowledge the existence of womens' neutral readings of texts that beckon male consumers. Some feminist scholars believe that when media texts feature an ideal subject position that hails male readers, women consumers either adopt the perspective of a "masculine reader" or identify with women in the text (e.g., Betterton, 1985; Doane, 1987; Mulvey, 1988). I have found no evidence of the former perspective, although there must be some lesbian and bisexual women consumers who create this reading of the swimsuit issue. But, some women do read the swimsuit issue as fashion and/or role models, which corresponds with the latter perspective.

Some of the women consumers who appreciate the swimsuit issue for its representation of fashion and/or role models write to *Sports Illustrated* to inquire about the swimwear displayed in the swimsuit issue. This reading occasionally appears in the Letters to the Editor section of *Sports Illustrated*. For example, in the February 16, 1970 issue, a woman writes that she wears the kind of swimsuits pictured in the swimsuit issue. In 1985 another woman pens that she "appreciates the public service" *Sports Illustrated* provides "by reminding your female readers to resume their exercise programs" (February 25, p. 76). Only one of the interviewed consumers articulates this reading. She says that she enjoys the swimsuit issue because of her professional interests as a model:

> I like to see updates in swimwear . . . I like to see the models and what kind of looks they have, that they're looking for in the industry . . . I like to look at their appearance . . . to see how they're doing their make-up now.

This consumer brings the swimsuit issues to her modeling school, where the students cut them up for an assignment that involves making a collage-picture book of "looks" with themes such as "romantic," "seductive," and "cute." She explains how she and other models at her school discuss the swimsuit issue:

> They look at the new models . . . "Oh my gosh, did you see that beautiful girl. She's gorgeous. I love her!" You know, "I love her hair . . . Kathy Ireland, she's beautiful." And then they keep up with her, you know, like, "Oh, she's doing this now, and she's doing that. I want to be just like her."

This consumer also sometimes cuts pictures out of the swimsuit issue and takes these pictures with her on shopping trips to find particular suits.

Although producers shape the swimsuit issue primarily for men to enjoy the representation of sexuality and beauty, and only secondarily for women to enjoy the representation of fashion and role models, some characteristics of the swimsuit issue texts encourage women to generate this reading. Media texts produced by *Sports Illustrated* suggest that if or when women read the swimsuit issue they attend to fashion or view the models as role models. For example, in one article in the 1989 swimsuit issue, the author highlights the stories of many men and only one woman who pin up pictures from the swimsuit issue, and he quotes this woman as saying "I'm not gay or anything— I just like the way they look . . . It's like an inspiration to me" (Newman, 1989, p. 228).

Women who see the swimsuit issue as representing role models for themselves, or women in general, build their reading upon the common denotative level meaning that the pictures represent ideally feminine and beautiful women. Consumers creating this reading attend to elements of the swimsuit issue text that signify the ideals or offer evidence of beauty management techniques. Earlier, I discussed the signifiers of hegemonic femininity and ideal beauty that appear in the swimsuit issue texts.

Women who appreciate the swimsuit issue for its representation of fashion focus on elements of the issue that signify fashion-related meaning. Obviously, these signifiers are present in the texts, because thirty-six percent of the interviewed consumers feel that the swimsuit issue conveys significant fashion-related meaning. Some interviewed consumers view the swimsuit issue as a medium for manufacturers to advertise their swimwear, while others say that the issue influences trends in the fashion world and/or stimulates the purchase of particular styles and brands.

There are several elements of the swimsuit issue texts that encourage consumers to see the issue as expressing fashion-related meaning. First, the models are from the fashion world. Second, the suits that appear in the swimsuit issue are created by many well-known designers/manufacturers and reflect the latest top-of-the-line styles. Third, the swimsuit issue features commentary on fashion. Often, captions, titles, and articles in the swimsuit issue (especially in the 1960s and 1970s) contain remarks about the fashion.[3] For example, a caption in the 1969 issue says, "At Sunset by the Mayaguez Hilton swimming pool, Erin shimmers in aluminum mesh. Giorgio Sant Angelus' creation covers Erin fully in front. The back consists mainly of thin straps" (p. 35). The captions and often the articles mention the swimwear manufacturers/designers and prices, and sometimes the articles note locations to purchase the suits. Finally, there are many similarities between the posing in the swimsuit issue and posing in women's fashion magazines. The three interviewed models and the interviewed modeling agent indicate that models use the same posing techniques for the swimsuit issue that they use for [other] fashion jobs, although other interviewed producers argue that the posing in the swimsuit issue is directed more toward the display of the models' bodies.

Although some elements of the swimsuit issue texts encourage consumers to view the issue as representing fashion and/or role models for women, there are many other elements of the texts which discourage this interpretation. As previously mentioned, women who read the issue in this manner must ignore, downplay, or reject two central components of the common denotative level meaning: that the issue is for men, and that the meaning of the issue is primarily related to sexuality. I have already discussed many parts of the swimsuit issue texts which encourage consumers to see the issue as a text about sexuality for men. I have also described some factors that discourage consumers from viewing the issue as fashion. Attending to textual signifiers, and influenced by prior socialization, consumers note that in many pictures you can barely see the swimwear, the suits are for women but the magazine suggests a male ideal subject position, and the swimsuit spread appears in a sports magazine rather than in a fashion magazine or catalog. In fact, fifty-four percent of the interviewed consumers feel that the swimsuit issue has very little or no relationship to fashion. Even those consumers who believe that there is a significant relationship between fashion and the swimsuit issue think that the theme of fashion is secondary to the common denotative meaning.

Representing signifiers of fashion-related meaning allows *Sports Illustrated* to claim a legitimate connection to the fashion world, which helps to enhance the respectability of the swimsuit issue. It also helps *Sports Illustrated* to secure further profits from some women consumers who are devoted to the hegemonic feminine ideal. On the other hand, producers cannot go too far in addressing these women consumers, as they would lose [much of] their male audience, so the swimsuit issue features only a small number of fashion signifiers.

Although the swimsuit issue is open to interpretations that it represents fashion and role models for women, a strong commitment to normative ideals of femininity and beauty and/or heavy involvement in the fashion world is necessary to generate this reading. There are many characteristics of contemporary United States society that encourage women to develop these commitments/involvements. Most significantly, images of ideal femininity, beauty, and fashion are pervasive in the mass media.

Most women who aspire to the hegemonic feminine ideal do not view a sports magazine as their primary source for images of the ideal, since many women's magazines contain these images. Yet, the swimsuit issue is probably attractive to some women because it is known to feature images of femininity that men enjoy. And many women continue to depend on men to affirm their legitimacy in the world. As J. Berger (1985) states, "Men look at women. Women watch themselves being looked at . . . The surveyor of woman in herself is male: the surveyed is female" (p. 47). In other words, women learn to visually inspect themselves and other women with men's interests in mind. Thus, some scholars maintain that masculine culture mediates between images of women and women readers, because (most) women internalize men's standards for femininity (e.g., Bartky, 1982; 1988; Root, 1984; Winship, 1987). When women are striving to resemble the hegemonic feminine ideal, they are allowed to scrutinize the bodies of other women because it is assumed that they are really looking at other women for men, not for themselves.

Hegemonic femininity serves as a complement to, or the "supporting actor" for, the hegemonic masculine ideal. This is why the most socially significant appearance of women in *Sports Illustrated* is in the swimsuit issue. It is logical that a magazine about hegemonic masculinity would feature images of hegemonic femininity to complement hegemonic masculinity. These images of women serve men, rather than challenging women's secondary position in the magazine or society. Later in the chapter, I will address the views of those who critique the hegemonic feminine ideal.

## Men Who Do Not Identify with Hegemonic Masculinity

Not all men and women read the swimsuit issue in ways that affirm devotion to hegemonic definitions of masculinity and femininity. Some men create a neutral reading of the swimsuit issue, and thus fail to tap its potential to reinforce their masculine status. Five of the interviewed male consumers (twenty-five percent of the men) articulate this reading of the swimsuit issue. As one interviewed male consumer puts it, "I just don't get into that." Another interviewed male consumer remarks, "I'm actually fairly neutral about it. It doesn't offend me, and I'm not a big enough fan to plunk down a buck and a half to buy it myself."

Nothing in the swimsuit issue texts encourage male consumers to produce a neutral reading of the issue. In fact, to create this reading, men must ignore or reject textual suggestions inside and outside of the swimsuit issue that nature compels their attraction to and enjoyment of the swimsuit issue. Thus, this reading derives its inspiration from the social environment.

Access to critical frameworks of thought is not the source of neutral readings of the swimsuit issue, because when consumers view the issue from a critical perspective they create an oppositional reading rather than a neutral one. Neutral readings by men probably emerge from differing conceptions of what constitutes one's own masculinity or sexual identity. Men who are gay or do not define themselves according to normative masculine standards, and are not familiar or comfortable with an explicit critical framework, may simply have no interest in the swimsuit issue because it does not seem to speak to them.

It is not surprising that some men react in neutral ways to the swimsuit issue and other sexual representations of women. After all, the components of hegemonic masculinity are always in flux, and the ideal of masculinity can take many forms. For example, some men view masculinity primarily in terms of gender differences in cognitive styles. Of course, obtaining masculine status is not important to all men. I believe that men who neglect to pursue this status serve the feminist cause, although often not self-consciously.

Interestingly, a neutral reading represents one position in an implicit debate among men about the proper definition of normative masculinity. One side seems to view (mandatory) heterosexuality as a pivotal component of masculinity. They usually loudly applaud the swimsuit issue and other sexual representations of women to publicly confirm their own heterosexual status. On the other hand, many men who read the swimsuit issue and other sexual representations of women in a neutral way seem to view heterosexuality as less relevant or irrelevant to their conceptions of masculinity.

Men who create neutral readings of the swimsuit issue indirectly challenge the assumption that natural and universal heterosexuality compels all men to enjoy sexual representations of women, so men who produce this reading leave themselves open to questions about their heterosexual status. So, as previously mentioned, when some men articulate a neutral (or critical) reading of the swimsuit issue, they call attention to their heterosexual status. On the other hand, when men who create a neutral (or critical) reading do not scramble to announce heterosexual status, their reading represents at least partial opposition to hegemonic masculinity. Men, and women, can make their challenge to hegemonic masculinity more explicit by creating a feminist reading of the swimsuit issue.

### Feminists Who Criticize Hegemonic Femininity and Masculinity

Most feminists view the swimsuit issue as sexist. Thirty-eight percent of the interviewed consumers articulate this reading. Feminists hold different views about the degree to which the swimsuit issue reflects and reinforces sexism. For example, one interviewed consumer asserts that the swimsuit issue is "very sexist" and that she is "really adamant about it." At the other end of the spectrum, another interviewed consumer who labels the swimsuit issue "sexist" dissociates herself from feminists who assert stronger opinions by saying:

> I don't feel that strongly about it, 'cause I know my husband will look at it. It doesn't bother me that he looks at it or anything. I don't know, I don't know . . . I mean, it doesn't bother me *that* much.

Consumers who view the swimsuit issue as sexist articulate two interrelated complaints. First, they maintain that *Sports Illustrated* treats women differently than men. Feminists who articulate this complaint point to three interconnected problems: *Sports Illustrated* caters to male readers rather than both male and female readers, presents sexual images of women rather than sexual images of both women and men, and covers mainly men's sports rather than covering men's and women's sports in an equitable fashion. Earlier, I presented quotations from feminist consumers who articulate all three of these points.

Second, they argue that the swimsuit issue reinforces injurious versions of femininity and masculinity. These consumers assert that the swimsuit issue reinforces a version of femininity that emphasizes the appearance and sexuality of women while ignoring other parts of their lives. As one letter writer puts it, the swimsuit issue represents the stereotype of "woman as sexy broad" (February 12, 1973, p.78). An interviewed consumer states, "To me, it emphasizes women's sexuality as opposed to women's intellectuality, or even their involvement in sport itself . . . I have a problem with that." These consumers feel that the combination of tokenistic coverage of women athletes and the publication of the swimsuit issue by *Sports Illustrated* reinforces male dominance in sport, because it defines women's place in sport as display for men rather than as athletes. For example, one interviewed consumer contends that this combination "sends the message that women should be on the beach in swimsuits, not playing a particular sport." Of course, defining women in terms of their aesthetic and sexual appeal is not unique to *Sports Illustrated*. When women are represented in the popular media, producers often highlight their appearance and sexual appeal rather than other characteristics. This contributes to the widespread societal practice of defining and treating women on the basis of their appearance.

Feminist consumers complain that the swimsuit issue plays a part in pressuring women to wear themselves out trying to meet the current appearance ideal. One interviewed consumer maintains that the swimsuit issue:

> . . . shows how American society views women, as to how they *should* be and how they *should* look and how they *should* act and what they *should* wear . . . I mean, they're supposed to look glamorous and sexy. And, I'm not. I don't like to be portrayed that way at all . . . When I look at those magazines, it's like, "I'm supposed to be this way?" And [this image] is so popularized . . . [I think the swimsuit issue shows] just how society thinks how a woman should be today. Slim figure, not a stomach, long legs, and you know all the rest.

The outpouring of images of glamorized women featured in the popular media influences popular conceptions of ideal appearance. Women experience a great deal of pressure to conform to media-related ideals. In the United States, we even tend to believe that women have a moral obligation to conform to, or strive to meet, this beauty ideal (e.g., Caputi, 1983; Coward, 1985; Freedman, 1986; Lakoff & Scherr, 1984). Contrarily, people frequently view men as effeminate if they display a great deal of public concern with their own appearance. Many women spend an inordinate amount of time trying to shape their appearances to fit the current beauty ideal to gain male approval. As a result, they often neglect to dedicate adequate time to developing or using parts of themselves that would enable them to acquire more power relative to men, such as intellect and physical agility/strength. I believe that the contemporary beauty ideal is *the* central component of hegemonic femininity, because this ideal reflects and reinforces dichotomous notions of physical gender difference.

Feminists link criticisms of hegemonic femininity to a critique of hegemonic masculinity when they complain that the swimsuit issue plays a part in encouraging men to view women primarily in terms of their appearance and sexual appeal. As Freedman (1986) states, "Socialized to view females as the fair sex, men have learned to respond to contrived symbols of beauty" (p. 58). One interviewed consumer contends that the swimsuit issue, and other sexual representations of women, reinforce "the whole role that men are taught," where "women are playthings." Another interviewed consumer describes what she views as the ultimate results of what men learn:

I think [of the swimsuit issue as having] a broader meaning for all women. We're talking about . . . sexual harassment in the workplace, rapes are up how much all over the country, the attitude towards women seems to be going from bad to worse, and I really do think that these kinds of things all add to it. I think the psyche of men is at an all-time low where women are concerned. I think it's more anti-female out there than it's ever been before. And I think that these kinds of magazines, under the surface, really add to that.

There is a complex and non-deterministic interrelationship between representations designed to signify sexuality and actual sexual behavior. Nevertheless, most contemporary sexual representation features narrow versions of sexuality, and thus only affirms particular forms of sexual desire. This representation helps to fashion and naturalize the currently hegemonic form of heterosexuality (e.g., Dyer, R., 1985; Kinsman, 1987; Walkerdine, 1984). These texts encourage women to be sexually attractive but passive, while encouraging men to assert and pursue their sexual desires (e.g., Coward, 1985; Root, 1984; Winship, 1984). Litewka (1977) argues that many popular photographic texts encourage men and boys to fixate on particular parts of women that the texts define as sexual. These representations play a part in naturalizing men's practice of gazing at women in a way that defines women primarily in sexual terms. Certainly, encouraging men to view women in this unidimensional way does not foster the development of equality between women and men.

Feminist critiques of *Sports Illustrated* generally, and its swimsuit issue in particular, need to address the contemporary components of hegemonic masculinity. As feminists of both genders attempt to reduce aggression and violence that injures women and men, those who support hegemonic masculinity help to produce this violence, in sport, homes, and wars. As feminists strive to obtain opportunities for women to enter the arenas where they can develop and/or use physical strength and agility and to diminish the negative experiences of physically weak and uncoordinated men, those who endorse hegemonic masculinity bar women from these arenas and harass men who lack strength and agility. As socialists act to enhance collective concern for all people, the type of competitiveness advocated by those who champion hegemonic masculinity discourages concern for others. As activists in the gay/lesbian movement work against the widespread heterosexism in the United States, those who promote hegemonic masculinity reinforce this heterosexism in ways that damage the lives of gays, lesbians, bisexuals, and even heterosexuals. Finally, as feminists maneuver to obtain more overall power for women, those who uphold hegemonic masculinity attempt to deny women equal power. The current hegemonic masculine ideal, and practices that reinforce this ideal, play a role in maintaining the current gender order and generating barriers to gender equality. It is for these reasons that the type of masculinity featured in *Sports Illustrated* is politically dangerous.

Most of the interviewed producers declare that interpreting the swimsuit issue as sexist is simply inaccurate. So, it is not surprising that *Sports Illustrated* texts do little to encourage consumers to create feminist readings of the swimsuit issue. Feminist consumers know that *Sports Illustrated* and its swimsuit issue beckon male consumers, but they critique the idea that the magazines should be designed for men. These consumers also believe that the swimsuit issue texts urge them to view the models as ideally feminine, yet they critique the hegemonic feminine ideal.

Even in the Letters to the Editor section of *Sports Illustrated*, producers rarely publish comprehensive critiques from those who see the swimsuit issue as reinforcing injurious versions of femininity and masculinity. Perhaps the fact that producers exclude long letters from this section limits the usefulness of this forum for those who articulate thorough feminist critiques. As one interviewed producer puts it, long letters "don't stand much of a chance" of getting published in *Sports Illustrated*. Producers also do not publish letters if they seem "irate," an additional factor that might contribute to an underrepresentation of letters that feature (some) feminist perspectives. For the most part, consumer contact with comprehensive feminist critiques of the swimsuit issue occurs outside of mainstream media discourse, through reading the "alternative press" or talking with other people.

To create the reading that the swimsuit issue reinforces injurious versions of femininity and/or masculinity, consumers need to employ a feminist perspective. A variety of social experiences move consumers to develop a feminist perspective. An interviewed gay male consumer attributes his feminist views partly to his sexual orientation. He feels that his sexual orientation helps to make him aware that producers create the swimsuit issue for "straight males," because there are no "guys with g-strings out there." An interviewed Native-American consumer grew up on a reservation where she says she "wasn't really aware of mainstream culture" and "of the issues of how women were presented and how they were viewed" by people in this culture. She explains that now that she attends college outside the reservation, she has learned that people in United States society represent women as "sex objects" and expect women to look and behave in ways that she views as a problem. Now she criticizes these dominant societal expectations for women and representations such as the swimsuit issue which she feels legitimate these expectations. Another interviewed consumer describes a similar story: experiences at college led him to change his views and to perceive the swimsuit issue as sexist. He says that prior to college, in his teens, he was a "sexist pig" who viewed the swimsuit issue as "very attractive." An interviewed middle-aged consumer notes that at about twenty years old she thought that the women in the swimsuit issue were "pretty women" and that "nobody's forcing them to pose," but as her "political awareness and growth as a feminist . . . progressed" through involvement in the feminist movement she came to view the issue as sexist.

## Backlash against the Feminist Readings

The backlash against the changes initiated by civil rights movements of the 1960s and 1970s encourages antagonistic reactions to feminist arguments versus the swimsuit issue. Many male consumers who enjoy the swimsuit issue accuse feminists who critique the issue of "political correctness," of taking the issue much too seriously and being "party-poopers." Thus, many of the male writers whose affirmations of the swimsuit issue appear in *Sports Illustrated* use humor in an attempt to discredit feminist criticisms of the swimsuit issue. For example, in 1976 a writer expresses a series of questions about the models' athletic abilities such as, "Christie is a doll but can she consistently hit seven-footers," and then he asks, "Who cares" (February 2, p. 78)? In 1980 another man pens, "For all those women's libbers who dislike the bathing-suit issue—Well, I hope they get drafted" (March 3, p. 24). In response to the commonly appearing cancel-my-subscription letters, some men write to say that *Sports Illustrated* should *not* cancel, or should extend, their subscriptions.

Producers of *Sports Illustrated* also react to feminist criticisms of the swimsuit issue. Scholars observe that media producers employ a variety of strategies to deal with the criticism that they draw from media consumers and interest groups. These strategies include: admitting the legitimacy of complaints that can be easily dealt with without major changes and then making minor changes to address these complaints, delegitimating complaints by declaring that they affront basic American values, presenting changes as a response to public wishes rather than as a response to specific interest groups (Turow, 1984), coopting challenges by stripping them of their critical edge and melting them into mainstream discourse, and trivializing complaints (Ellsworth, 1984).

The producers of *Sports Illustrated* have employed several of these strategies. These producers addressed anti-racist critiques, which are discussed in the next chapter, by using token African-American models in the magazine, but they have not included representative numbers of models of color or modified the racist beauty standard that they use to select (most of) the models. These producers have also attempted to diminish feminist critiques of the swimsuit issue. As already mentioned, occasionally they include pictures of men in the Letters to the Editor section in response to liberal feminist complaints, but they have not put pictures of (lone) men into the swimsuit spread itself. This response acknowledges heterosexual women readers who want to see sexual images of men, but refuses to treat these readers as equal to heterosexual men. In some swimsuit issue articles, the authors repudiate the feminist arguments and portray rebelling against others to defend or look at the issue as fun. *Sports Illustrated* editors frame criticism of the swimsuit issue in the Letters to the Editor section in a way that weakens and deflects much of the feminist criticism. For example, in 1970 the editors placed the title "Liberated Librarians" in the Letters to the Editor section (February 16, p. 66). This title affirms the woman librarian who wrote to say that she wears the type of swimwear that appears in the swimsuit issue. Through the use of this title producers portray her as a "feminist" and simultaneously define feminism as advocating the freedom to display more flesh. Because the meaning suggested by this title does not coincide with most feminist arguments, the title actually works to diminish feminist critiques.

*Sports Illustrated* regularly prints letters from writers who trivialize the concerns of those who link their complaints about the swimsuit issue to their complaints about coverage of women's sport. In these letters, the writers dub the swimsuit issue models as "Sportswoman of the Year," argue that the models are athletic, and propose that producers picture women athletes in the swimsuit spread.[4] Also, one of the interviewed producers says that she sends individual responses to those who connect disapproval of the swimsuit issue to grievances about *Sports Illustrated*'s coverage of women's sport. She notes:

[I send out] a listing of what we've covered in the area of sports particular to women in the last year . . . I give them a fairly complete listing of our major stories and our cover references to try to show that this perception that we are only covering women once a year in swimsuits is untrue . . . This is the one misconception that comes out at swimsuit time . . . And, I always know it's coming. Otherwise, we don't really get complaints about our sports coverage. I mean, I think everybody realizes that we cover everything.

Scarcely anyone believes that *Sports Illustrated* does not cover women's sports at all, but many feminists feel that the magazine covers women's sports in a tokenistic manner. Thus, this response oversimplifies and trivializes the feminist critique.

From the perspective of fans and producers of *Sports Illustrated*, feminists have "stepped out of line." Feminists straightforwardly challenge the pursuit of masculine status by consumers and indirectly challenge the pursuit of profit by producers. Unlike the women who complement the hegemonic masculine project and the women who attempt to stay out of the gender debate altogether, feminists pose a threat to the gender order. So, both producers and *Sports Illustrated* fans try to put feminists "in their place." Joining the general backlash against feminism, these producers and fans defend *Sports Illustrated* and thus hegemonic masculinity itself.

# Hegemonic Masculinity Built on the Backs of People of Color

Despite the fact that many feminists critique the ideals of femininity and masculinity that are associated with the swimsuit issue, most fail to criticize the racist nature of these ideals. It is crucial that feminists address racism, because hegemonic masculinity and femininity are built upon a foundation of racism.

Only a few letters published in *Sports Illustrated* feature the argument that the swimsuit issue is racist, and these letters did not appear in *Sports Illustrated* until the 1980s. Although this reading is rarely presented in the mainstream media, it is clear that some consumers view the swimsuit issue from an anti-racist perspective.

## *Racism as a Central Component of Hegemonic Femininity*

Some consumers complain that the swimsuit issue features an under-representation of women of color as models. These consumers see this underrepresentation as evidence of racial discrimination against models of color. They argue that this discrimination is caused by a racially-biased beauty ideal, which eulogizes only the appearance of women with European ancestry. These consumers explain that this discrimination reinforces the racially-biased appearance standards in society. Indeed, scholars point out that mainstream beauty standards in most Western cultures (which media images help to shape) reflect and reinforce societal racism (e.g., Fishburn, 1982; Gardner, 1980; Joseph, 1981). One of the interviewed consumers articulated this reading, speculating on how this discrimination might affect women of color:

> They don't have . . . people [of color] in [the swimsuit issue] . . . I mean for a black female or an Asian female or a Native-American female, . . . I think . . . it can make them feel like, "Maybe we aren't as beautiful as the other white females in the magazine."

Some people of color critique mainstream beauty standards, while others internalize the racist ideals. Some people of color use plastic surgery, hair straighteners, and skin lighteners in an attempt to conform to these ideals (hooks, 1988; Lakoff & Scherr, 1984; Stedman, 1989).

The small number of women of color used as models in the swimsuit issue texts over the years encourages consumers to create this oppositional reading. In the late 1960s and the 1970s the swimsuit issues only occasionally featured one or two women of color, and these women tended to come from the shooting locale rather than travel with *Sports Illustrated* from the United States mainland. It was not until 1971 that a model with visible African ancestry appeared, and then not again until 1982. During the 1980s and early to mid-1990s the swimsuit issue featured models with African ancestry, yet these models typically possessed very light-color skin and facial features that conform to the Anglo-American beauty ideal. The first very dark model did not appear in the swimsuit issue until 1990. Generally, there were one and maybe two models of color in the swimsuit issues when they showed up at all. Amazingly, in the 1990 swimsuit issue the producers pictured four models of color. In 1996, a black model appeared on the cover of the swimsuit issue for the first time. The degree to which this cover counters (the usual) racism is limited by the fact that the black model stands alongside a white model, wears a suit with a leopard-skin design, has light-color skin, and has long, straight, light-colored hair that blows in the wind. The fact that this swimsuit issue was shot in South Africa probably affected the decision to feature both a black and white model on the cover, as picturing only a white model in the context of the most overtly racist society in the world probably would have elicited cries from consumers charging *Sports Illustrated* with racism.

Scholars have observed that when people of color appear as models in mainstream media texts, usually as tokens, they often have light-color skin and features that resemble the Western white ideal (e.g., Freedman, 1986; Lakoff & Scherr, 1984; Okazawa-Rey, Robinson & Ward, 1987). A recent trend in the modeling world is to use models with a so-called "ethnic" or "exotic" look. These models possess slightly darker skin than the traditional Western white ideal, because people think the darkness conveys an additional hint of sexuality (e.g., Banner, 1983; Howell, 1988; Stedman, 1989). But, as Lakoff and Scherr (1984) comment, the exotic look embraces those who are " . . . not white but whose features [are] close enough to white not to shock the sensibilities of mainstream Americans" (p. 270).

As already mentioned, even the features of the white swimsuit issue models provide evidence of a racist beauty ideal, as they usually have light-color and straight hair, and mostly have blue eyes. Commonly, since the mid-1970s, the white models have tanned skin. As previously discussed, darker skin is associated with the stereotype of blacks as more sexual. As Caputi (1983) points out, only whites can afford to get a tan, because they do not have to (for the most part) endure racism.

Written text in the swimsuit issue also extols the racially-biased beauty ideal, by complimenting physical features that many whites possess, such as blonde hair and blue eyes, while rarely even mentioning any of the features that people of color possess. For example, in the 1966 swimsuit issue the publisher says that the woman on the cover "would satisfy the qualifications for most magazine covers, being what she is—beautiful and blonde and blue-eyed" (p. 4). In 1978 the author of the Letter from the Publisher refers to, but neglects to criticize, a model's practice of squeezing limes over her head to make her hair bleach blonde. The 1989 swimsuit issue includes a statement about the enticing blonde hair and "good coloring" (p. 78) of one model, and a passage that portrays women from Sweden as particularly pretty.

Given the indisputable textual evidence that racially-biased standards of beauty influence the swimsuit issue, it is amazing how few people (publicly) argue that the issue is racist. Evidently, an anti-racist perspective is necessary to detect these biases and few possess such a perspective. The ways that people of color commonly appear in the mainstream media probably contribute to our inability to perceive the racial bias. Most of us are so well schooled in the dominant beauty ideal that we take it for granted, viewing it as natural, universal, and bias-free.

Tokenism does not solve the problem of racist beauty standards. Tokenism implies that one or two people of color can represent all people of color, an obviously insulting notion. Tokenism attempts to pacify the critics instead of creating actual change. In other words, media producers use tokenism to seem as if they care about people of color, but such limited coverage of people of color demonstrates that they really do not care. Nevertheless, most of us have learned to see tokenistic representation of people of color as evidence of absence of racism rather than evidence of racism.

Since the swimsuit issue models serve as societal exemplars of hegemonic femininity, their racial similarity suggests that the hegemonic feminine ideal itself is racist. There is a racial hierarchy among women, in terms of appearance. Women with white skin, blonde and straight hair, blue eyes and small noses are at the top, and women with dark skin, black and curly hair, and big noses are at the bottom. Even white women with dark hair, curly hair, big noses, and dark eyes are seen as inadequate. Women who conform to the ideal, or come close to conforming, can feel superior to other women simply because of their racial characteristics. This hierarchy affects women of color, who experience lowered self-esteem when they internalize this racist beauty ideal, and who may be subjected to appearance-based discrimination when others internalize this ideal.

The interviewed producers did not broach the topic of race, but I asked many of them about the complaints of some consumers prior to 1990 that *Sports Illustrated* neglected to include many models of color. Not all of the interviewed producers agreed that *Sports Illustrated* overlooked models of color. Most of the interviewed producers feel that *Sports Illustrated* in the past did not feature enough models of color, but they were quick to assert that *Sports Illustrated* has corrected this problem or that it currently works to eliminate this problem. "Well, I would agree with that [complaint] in earlier years, but I'd say in later years we've used a very fair number of women of color," maintains one interviewed producer. Another interviewed producer concurs with the complaint "to a degree," stating, "it's something we're aware of and we're doing our best to fix." Still another interviewed producer declares:

> It's about time. I can say honestly that it's long, long, long, long, long, long overdue . . . Finally, the woman of color is being appreciated for her actual beauty, and it just took [the producers] a lot longer to come to that appreciation, but now that they're doing it, I'm just happy.

Interestingly, many of the interviewed producers equate "people of color" with "African-Americans," ignoring the underrepresentation of Asian-Americans, Latina-Americans, and Native-Americans. In the popular media, producers commonly use African-Americans to represent all people of color (Robinson, 1985).

The interviewed producers cite a variety of reasons why so few models of color appear in past swimsuit issues: bad weather during the shoots with models of color, difficulty photographically exposing the models of color, not enough experienced black models with "swimsuit-type bodies" to choose from, the swimsuit issue reflecting trends in society and the mass media that excluded people of color, and fear that too few consumers would appreciate the look of these models. Here, an interviewed producer articulates two of these arguments:

> To tell you the truth, they're harder to expose. [It's] sometimes harder to get a better picture. Also, I think that there aren't as many black models that are . . . the sort of physical type that we need for bathing suit stuff. And, most of the really well known black models tend to be really tall [and] slender . . . They're wonderful and athletic and they're in our issue, but they're not often the kind of body type that we like in the [swimsuit issue], that fill out the bathing suit, that are bathing suit models, quote unquote.

Some of the interviewed producers also address the question of what led to the increase in the number of models of color in the swimsuit issue starting at about 1990. A few think that complaints by readers prompted the change. One producer asserts, "I think it's . . . good that people spoke up, because I know that that's what made the difference." Some producers believe that increased sensitivity of the producers or general societal changes resulted in the inclusion of more models of color. One producer puts it:

> Well, I think it's just growing up, the magazine's growing up, and being more aware of the social consequences of what it's do-ing . . . We're just sort of chugging along with the culture. And I think that we're reflecting it.

Finally, another interviewed producer describes a much more cynical reason:

> A lot of the different magazines . . . talk about the increased num-ber of ethnic populations just at large, and how advertisers need to start to incorporate make-up in a hundred and one different

shades, so that it includes the Latino community as well as the African-American community . . . for profit.

### Racism as a Central Component
### of Hegemonic Masculinity

The number of models of color that appear in the swimsuit issue is not just seen as discrimination against models of color, it is also seen as discrimination against [heterosexual] men of color. Some consumers complain that the swimsuit issue is a racist text because it fails to picture (enough) women that interest [heterosexual] men of color. One interviewed consumer articulates this reading, and begins to discuss how the racial discrimination might influence the thoughts of [heterosexual] men of color:

> I would think a majority [sic] of the readers [of *Sports Illustrated*] are black or Asian or whatever, but they don't have those people in [the swimsuit issue] . . . Say, for the black [male] athlete, maybe he's thinking, "Well, gee, I wonder if my girl can look this good in that particular swimsuit. Or maybe not," you know.

Consumers who create this reading usually assume that [heterosexual] men are primarily interested in women from their same racial category. In the United States, we have a long history of repression regarding interracial sexual relationships that still renders these relationships somewhat socially unacceptable. The most taboo relationship involves black men and white women, and the continued existence of the stereotype of black men as rapists reinforces this taboo (Davis, A. Y., 1983).

The swimsuit issue texts both encourage and discourage this reading. Textual suggestions that men should enjoy the swimsuit issue may serve as an impetus for some to create the reading that [heterosexual] male consumers of color also deserve to enjoy such representations. However, consumers who create this reading question textual suggestions that the swimsuit issue models represent ideal beauty, labeling the *Sports Illustrated* ideal as racist.

A variety of elements of the swimsuit issue texts imply a white ideal subject position, further urging consumers to view the swimsuit issue as a text that discriminates against consumers of color. For example, the 1965 swimsuit spread includes a comment about flesh-colored materials, omitting mention that the specified materials only resemble the flesh tone of whites. The 1984 swimsuit issue contains a picture that demonstrates insensitivity to the historical experiences of African-Americans. In this picture, a black boy looks at a white model who lies on a fruit stand at a market and wears a swimsuit that features the words "Cargo Africa 1944." The caption for this picture says that the black boy is "sold on her." In the 1989 swimsuit issue, the author of a travel article writes about vacationing in Mexico to become "bronze," a vacationing goal that mainly appeals to people of European descent. Finally, people of color most commonly show up in the swimsuit issue as part of the background, as "exotic" symbols of the shooting locale. For example, the 1989 swimsuit issue features a picture of a Native-American man, adorned in feathers on his arms and head, with his arms encircling a miniature image of two swimsuit issue models. *Sports Illustrated* and its swimsuit issues do not beckon consumers of color (Davis, L. R., 1993).

One interviewed producer believes that the recent inclusion of more models of color in the swimsuit issue indicates a shift toward considering men of color as an essential part of the audience. She states, "I would say that if they're including women of color, it's . . . to encourage men of color who are viewers, not just the white men that they've catered to kind of all along." This producer thinks that other producers probably initiated this change to increase profits.

*Sports Illustrated* tries to pursue a few extra dollars by appealing to [heterosexual] men of color with token models of color. This practice probably works to diminish the number, and intensity, of accusations of racism. But men of color are much less attractive to advertisers than white men, as the mean/median/collective income of men of color falls far short of that of white men. So, the magazine does not want to "go overboard" by featuring many models of color, particularly those who do not resemble the Anglo-appearance ideal, as the magazine might lose a significant proportion of their white audience and thus much profit. Due to thorough socialization, most white men (and many men of color) prefer the appearances of women who possess features that resemble the Anglo-ideal. Thus, although *Sports Illustrated* has begun to address heterosexual men of color, these men are only of secondary concern. The magazine completely ignores the interests of consumers of color who are women and gay men.

The widespread popularity of *Sports Illustrated* and its swimsuit issue mean that many people in the United States come in contact with *Sports Illustrated*'s version of hegemonic femininity and masculinity. This chapter illustrated how race influences these gender ideals. The magazine company enlarges its purse on the backs of people of color, as hegemonic masculinity and hegemonic femininity are defined in a racist way. Hegemonic femininity is associated with white women. Further, men of color still occupy a back seat relative to white men, in the hierarchy of masculinities, as the hegemonic masculine subject is defined as a white man. Men of color are not alone in the back seat, as they share this seat with many other people, including the entire (post)colonialized world.

# Hegemonic Masculinity
# Built on the Backs of
# "the (Post)Colonialized Other"

The difference between past and present forms of "colonialism" is that contemporary colonialism is more closely related to the symbolic realm. Of course, the material legacy of colonialism remains. Therefore, throughout this book, when I use the term "postcolonialized" countries, I put parentheses around the term "post" to emphasize the material nature of contemporary Western dominance of these countries. Colonizers still physically occupy some of these countries. And, although the original colonizers physically departed from most of these countries, many colonizers retain their influence over these countries in other ways, such as through politics, religion, the media, and especially economics.

In the past, the colonizer invaded the other's homeland, conquered the other with his army, occupied the other's homeland, ruled the other, and attempted to impose his culture on the other. In contrast, the contemporary symbolic colonizer arrives in the (post)colonialized world as an actual and media tourist. Those who can afford it often use their leisure time to travel to (post)colonialized lands as actual tourists, whereas people who cannot afford it become media tourists by consuming mediated representations of (post)colonialized lands. As I will illustrate, the phenomenon of contemporary symbolic colonialism perpetuates many characteristics of the colonial past.

In this chapter I use the swimsuit issue to demonstrate the link between the hegemonic masculine ideal and a colonialist mentality. The swimsuit issue, a masculinity-text par excellence, has cultural meanings that reflect and reinforce the practices of symbolic colonialism.

*The Hegemonic Masculine Subject as Actual and Media Tourist*

Although work in the public arena has been a defining characteristic
of United States hegemonic masculinity, leisure also contributes to the
masculine complex.[1] In order to retain a masculine aura away from
work, men from all classes pursue leisure activities that are dominated
by men and/or associated with masculine traits such as violence, strength,
competitiveness, and achievement. As more and more women assume
jobs in the public arena and engage in a wider range of leisure activities, a more narrow range of jobs and leisure activities can be used to
secure a masculine reputation. *Sports Illustrated*, as an exemplar of the
current hegemonic masculine ideal, promotes a societal ideal of masculinity that encompasses play.

Sports Illustrated *Readers Defining Masculinity*
*through Leisure*

Since people from the United States tend to associate sport with leisure,
it seems logical that *Sports Illustrated* itself is associated with leisure.
Although sport can serve as a break from work, many men take their
actual or mediated sport consumption very seriously; thus "real sport
fans" may even need a break from "the serious world of sport."

The swimsuit issue is allied with leisure, as it is seen as a break
from "the serious" elements of life.[2] A few of the interviewed producers
see this meaning as central to the purpose of the swimsuit issue,
defining the issue as a "diversion," "entertainment," and a break or
"change of pace" from the regular sports coverage. The interviewed
producers also indicate that they design the swimsuit issue to convey
an attitude that one might have while engaged in play or leisure. As
one interviewed producer expresses it, they shape the issue to communicate "vitality," and "to lift the spirits of the readers and give them a
sense of . . . fun and excitement."

Certain features of the texts produced by *Sports Illustrated* encourage the view that the swimsuit issue should be associated with play or
a playful attitude. As already mentioned, the models sometimes pose
in ways that suggest that they are engaged in play or in ways that
signify childhood, a period of life we associate with play. The backgrounds and props commonly exhibited in the swimsuit spreads also
suggest themes related to sport and play. Such props include: colorful
boats, swimming goggles, scuba gear, surfboards, and towels. Beaches
and pools often are visible in the background of the pictures. A light-

hearted and playful reading is encouraged by extensive use of humor, wordplay, and entertaining stories in the written parts of the swimsuit issue. The usual publication of humorous responses to criticism in the Letter to the Editor section of *Sports Illustrated* further urges consumers to view the issue from a playful perspective and to characterize critics of the issue as "too serious."

The joking tone used by many male consumers who enjoy the swimsuit issue indicates that many consumers do in fact respond playfully to the issue. For example, the writer of a 1968 Letter to the Editor says, "Thank you for making a cold Wisconsin 'bareable' " (January 30, p. 68), and the writer of a 1986 letter exclaims, "Help! My heart just stopped. Could Kathy Ireland administer CPR? Please" (February 24, p. 77).

Since *Sports Illustrated* represents a standard for current definitions of hegemonic masculinity, the magazine can be seen as encouraging men to fashion their masculinity through their leisure practices rather than through their work. But leisure in *Sports Illustrated* is not simply characterized as consumption of sport and sexual representations of women. Over the years, *Sports Illustrated* has also featured tourism as an important leisure activity. Contemporary men can be actual participants in tourism or simply consume media images of tourism.

## Sports Illustrated *Readers as Tourists*

One cannot comprehend the world of contemporary tourism without understanding how photography is central to this world. Mass produced travel photography influences what tourists see, how they see it, and how they understand what they see (Albers & James, 1988; Urry, 1990). As Urry (1990) states:

> Involved in much tourism is a kind of hermeneutic circle. What is sought for in a holiday is a set of photographic images, as seen in tour company brochures or on TV programmes. While the tourist is away, this then moves on a tracking down and capturing of these images for oneself. And it ends up with travellers demonstrating that they really have been there by showing their version of the images that they had seen originally before they set off. Photography is thus intimately bound up with the tourist gaze. (p. 140)

The *Sports Illustrated* swimsuit issue features pictures that reflect the practices of contemporary tourist photography.

Although textual analysis of early issues of *Sports Illustrated* reveals that the swimsuit issue originated at least partially in media coverage of tourism, nowadays most of the interviewed producers do not see tourism as central to the meaning of the issue. At most, they view tourism as a minor theme in the swimsuit issue. Influential producers agree that, "There's no particular link between [the swimsuit issue] and any desire or interest in stimulating tourism." Thus, it appears that the *Sports Illustrated* producers do not *directly* promote tourism.

Yet, tourism is fundamental to the meaning of the swimsuit issue. It influences the selection of sites for each annual issue. The producers usually choose sites that are common United States tourist destinations. In 1991, producers made the connection between the swimsuit issue and tourism/vacationing even more explicit by taking the pictures on cruise-boat lines rather than in specific countries.

Urry (1990) notes that tourist sites vary in the degree of prestige associated with them. Prestige rises as fewer and more wealthy travelers are associated with the site. *Sports Illustrated* producers define the ideal swimsuit issue shooting locale in regard to the ability and desire of United States residents to visit the place. It seems that they attempt to achieve a balance between places many tourists might go to and places where only the most wealthy tourists can visit. One interviewed producer describes ideal places as "far" and not "well traveled," yet an "up and coming new place for tourists to go . . . It has to be some new and different place that's still considered a great place to visit."

Several of the interviewed producers mention that the selected sites are usually warm and tropical locations. As one interviewed producer puts it, *Sports Illustrated* goes to "tropical places, where people want to be in February when the issue comes out, rather than wherever they are." They design the swimsuit issue to provide a "change of pace" for and brighten the winter of people who live in colder climates. The sites most commonly featured in the swimsuit issue texts are (post)colonialized countries, such as the Dominican Republic and Mexico, and occasionally places in the southern United States, such as Florida and southern California.

In addition to the shooting locations, the backgrounds and props that show up in the swimsuit spreads also suggest themes related to typical United States tourist destinations. Usual backgrounds include beaches, tropical plants and trees, sunrises, and sunsets. Pools, ornate buildings, islands, and grass-roofed huts also frequently appear in the background.

The written text in the swimsuit issues further intimates that the issues promote tourism. Most of the time the text that accompanies the swimsuit issue pictures includes the name of the location of the shoot, but other times this text goes even further and directly mentions vacationing or tourist-related information. In the 1960s and 1970s, the captions often contained the names of particular resorts, hotels, or other establishments. The most blatant sign of promotion is that the swimsuit issues usually feature an article on vacation, adventure, or sport in the location of the shoot. Often these articles describe practical matters such as accommodations and transportation. The authors of these articles also commonly discuss popular vacation activities in the shooting locale, such as swimming and tanning at a beach, fishing, golf, and scuba diving.

Apparently there is no financial relationship between *Sports Illustrated* and the host countries, but there is an interesting relationship between the swimsuit issue producers, (potential) host countries, and the tourism industry. The swimsuit issue employees receive a large amount of mail from businesses located in, and representatives of, countries who would like *Sports Illustrated* to select their country as a site for the swimsuit issue. One interviewed producer explains that various people connected to tourism "try to lure [*Sports Illustrated*] into coming to some new and hot spot where a new hotel has just been built, [or] some place where they're trying to get more publicity for." It is unclear exactly how the swimsuit issue producers respond to this solicitation. According to the interviewed producers, *Sports Illustrated* usually initiates contact with representatives from the countries the magazine chooses as sites for the swimsuit issue. As one interviewed producer points out, "We contact them. We are too big and too important to be dictated to by a public relations agency." Representatives of the selected countries often assist the swimsuit issue employees as they plan and conduct the shoot. In fact, swimsuit issue producers often use these contacts to hire a guide from the host country to aid the crew while they are on location. Despite the lack of intent to promote tourism, some of the interviewed producers state that when they pick a particular country, representatives from this country seem pleased and view the swimsuit issue as a form of publicity. As one interviewed producer observes, "It makes tremendous publicity for the place . . . It's quite valuable for tourism."

The swimsuit issues contain many pictures and written texts that mix signifiers of tourism with signifiers of nature, sport, and sexuality.

This is not surprising since nature, sport, and sex tourism are three types of tourism that have been advertised recently in United States media.

As already mentioned, when *Sports Illustrated* includes an article about vacationing in the shooting locale, they often discuss sporting activities the tourist may want to pursue while visiting this locality. Sometimes *Sports Illustrated* even substitutes an article about sport in the shooting location for an article about vacationing. In fact, many people in the tourist industry now use sporting events and activities to lure tourists, especially wealthy men, to various countries (e.g., Kang, 1988; Manning, 1977; Renson & Careel, 1986).

The swimsuit issues often feature local flora and fauna in the background of the pictures and describe local flora and fauna in the written texts. The practice of people from urban and highly industrialized societies pursuing nature-tourism probably encourages *Sports Illustrated* to highlight nature in this way. Even armchair nature enthusiasts consume pictures of the "wilderness" of faraway lands (Haraway, 1989; Nash, 1979).

Advertisements for tourism in many (post)colonialized countries often portray women native to these countries in a highly sexualized manner (Courtney & Whipple, 1983), and some actually promote sex tourism in these countries (e.g., Enloe, 1983; Thitsa, 1981; Wood, 1984). Sometimes the swimsuit issues picture residents of the shooting locations in ways that signify eroticism. But more often, the eroticism associated with the shooting locales is transposed onto the bodies of the swimsuit issue models. How the swimsuit issues convey sexual meaning through the representation of symbols of (post)colonialized countries will be discussed later in this chapter.

Although most consumers do not see tourism as central to the meaning of the swimsuit issue, some consumers do. Printed letters to the editor sometimes address the pictured location. For example, in 1985, one writer comments that the swimsuit issue pictures "captured" "the wonderful variety of landscapes in Australia" (March 4, p. 80). Both producers and consumers indirectly link the swimsuit issue with tourism when they state that looking at the swimsuit issue amounts to a break from the winter weather they are experiencing, something only traveling to a tropical region can actually do. A common theme in printed letters to the editor contrasts the writer's winter environment to the warm lands displayed in the swimsuit issue pictures, and the writer often declares that the pictures will help him endure the winter. For example, one writer notes that, "The swimsuit issue melted the snow here in Pennsylvania" (February 22, 1982, p. 72). In this case, looking at the swimsuit issue becomes a substitute for actual travel to a tropical destination.

*Sports Illustrated* readers are not only media tourists, but many are actual tourists. In a 1988 study of the magazine's national edition subscribers (Don Bowden Associates, 1988), the researchers report that 43.4 percent of these subscribers flew to another country for pleasure in the prior three years. During that period, 19 percent went to Hawaii, 16.2 percent to Mexico, 4.6 percent to Bermuda, 8.9 percent to Bahamas, 4.4 percent to Puerto Rico, and 14 percent to another Caribbean island. At the very least, the swimsuit issue contributes to the creation of what John Urry (1990) calls "the tourist gaze." Urry (1990) maintains that, "To be a tourist is one of the characteristics of 'modern' experience" (p. 4). The tourist gaze involves examination of what we regard as "out of the ordinary" with an attitude of "interest and curiosity" (p. 1).

## "The (Post)colonialized Other" as Exotic Spectacle for the Hegemonic Masculine Subject

*Sports Illustrated* producers presume that consumers of the swimsuit issue are spectators of the "exotic." Many of the interviewed producers indicate that *Sports Illustrated* uses the criteria of "exoticism" to help them select the country for the shoot, the specific backdrops for the pictures, and the pictures that will eventually appear in the magazine. For example, one interviewed producer says that when *Sports Illustrated* determines the site for the shoot they choose "the most exotic thing they can find for the year." In selecting backdrops, producers try to pick backgrounds that "give a feeling of" the "pretty exotic" shooting locales.

I asked the interviewed producers to describe what they meant by "exotic." "Exotic" means "something they haven't done before," one producer explains. Another producer says it means "surprising," a place that "you've never heard of," and a place that includes "things that are unusual." A third interviewed producer defines exotic places as those that feature people with "cultural backgrounds" that "clash" with the culture of people from the United States. Thus, one goal of the swimsuit issue is to survey the culturally different. As one interviewed producer puts it, "I think that doing the swimsuit issue in an exotic place gives us an opportunity to discover something about a culture, . . . and appreciate it and examine it."

### The Other Is Culturally Different from the Western Self

Much of contemporary tourism is based on the premise that people from the (post)colonialized world are vastly different from the culturally known Western self (e.g., Albers & James, 1988; Beloff, 1985; van den

Berghe & Keyes, 1984). Perceived cultural differences have become *the* central tourist attraction. Contemporary tourism involves the commodification and marketing of ethnicity, where travel agents sell ethnic stereotypes as marks of ethnicity for tourists to seek (Adams, 1984; van den Berghe & Keyes, 1984; Williamson, 1986).

While Western tourists search for "the authentic" cultural meaning of the people who reside in the sites that they visit, many people who live in tourist localities stage performances for the tourist, manufacturing the illusion of authenticity. In this age of tourism, ethnicity exists as a newly created or recreated phenomenon that people often shape in ways that reflect popular historical myth. This method of defining ethnicity works to homogenize, decontextualize, and mythologize groups of people and their cultures in the interests of commodity-oriented leisure (e.g., Albers & James, 1988; MacCannell, 1984; van den Berghe & Keyes, 1984). As MacCannell (1984) explains, two apparently contradictory tendencies underlie contemporary tourism, " . . . the international homogenization of the culture of tourists and the artificial preservation of local ethnic groups so that they can be consumed as tourist experiences" (p. 387). Images in the swimsuit issues mirror the world of contemporary tourism.

The swimsuit issue producers employ a variety of practices to convey a country's "flavor." For example, they select shooting locations that feature types of architecture and boats that symbolize the culture of the host country. They also picture non-Western wildlife, such as camels. The swimsuit issue texts suggest that consumers should regard this wildlife as spectacle for the travelers' enjoyment. For example, in the 1989 swimsuit issue, a spread of pictures in Kenya signify a safari theme through the title, captions, clothing that resembles safari outfits, and elephants in the background.

Producers sometimes include people who they view as symbolizing the "host" culture in the swimsuit issue pictures, usually in the background. Sometimes producers spontaneously ask local people near a photographic shoot to appear in the pictures, whereas other times they prearrange the presence of "local people." Sometimes the "local residents" pose, while other times producers claim to depict them engaged in their daily activities. Producers commonly picture pre-adolescent boys from the (post)colonialized shooting locations, who are seen playing with the model, providing a service for her, or simply helping to decorate the picture. Producers also picture grown men from (post)colonialized countries. These men almost always show up in the background, busy at work or providing a service for the model. In the late 1980s, the swimsuit issues contained three pictures that feature girls from (post)colonialized countries. In these pictures, the girls wear fancy traditional costumes and interact with the model either as performers or playmates. In the late 1980s, the swimsuit issues also included three pictures that depict women from (post)colonialized countries. These pictures seem to highlight differences between the Western models and the native women. In two of these pictures, the native women have on clothing that covers most of their bodies while the models wear skimpy bathing suits. In the third picture, the model imitates the activity of the native woman, carrying a basket of food on her head.

The swimsuit issues commonly depict people from (post)colonialized countries engaged in activities considered unusual in the Western world, such as paddling a boat with coconut shells or standing guard in costume and paint while playing a flute-like instrument. Sometimes producers picture people from these countries performing culturally-specific forms of entertainment for the model. For example, one picture features several little girls dressed in grass skirts and breastplates, and the caption identifies these girls as dancers.

Generally speaking, the authors of written texts in the swimsuit issues imply that people from (post)colonialized countries are vastly different from Westerners. For example, two swimsuit issue captions describe people from the (post)colonialized countries as amazed at the model's swimsuits (1988; 1989). Producers also evoke cultural difference by employing stereotypes of the (post)colonialized countries, such as in the 1989 issue where the caption for a picture taken in Mexico reads, "Bring on the mariachis and break out the guacamole . . ." (p. 235).

*Sports Illustrated* is similar to many other Western-produced media texts, because in representing people from the non-Western world as exotic spectacle for an audience,[3] it suggests a Western ideal subject position (e.g., Davis, L. R., 1993; Desnoes, 1985; Said, 1978; Williamson, 1986). Popular Western media texts often use the (post)colonialized countryside as exotic backdrop for Western adventures, fantasies, and tests of manhood (e.g., Alloula, 1986; Desnoes, 1988; Scott, 1989). Authors of the written texts in the swimsuit issue beckon Western consumers when they imply that the (post)colonialized countries featured in the issue are ideal places to travel rather than places of residence. The fact that the authors of the swimsuit issue texts present a version of history that privileges a pro-colonialist perspective, a matter that will be discussed later, also hails Western consumers. Finally, the portrayal of (post)colonialized countries as the antithesis of the Western world intimates that ideal spectators of the swimsuit issue come from the West.

In fact, the audience of *Sports Illustrated* does mainly dwell in the Western world. A study of the paid circulation of *Sports Illustrated* on

February 4, 1991 (Audit Bureau of Circulation, 1991) found that ninety-six percent of the readers reside in the United States, and most of the other readers live in Canada.

Thus, *Sports Illustrated*, as a vehicle that features an exemplar of the current hegemonic masculine ideal, reinforces a version of masculinity that is distinctly Western. Non-Westerners are viewed as vastly different from the Western masculine self and thus as objects for scrutiny.

So far I have discussed the notion of representing difference from the West without specifying what kind of difference I am talking about. How do the swimsuit issue texts characterize the (post)colonialized other, and what does this imply about the Western hegemonic masculine ideal?

### The Other Is "Black," So the Self Is White

When the pictures in the swimsuit issues contain people other than the models, most of the time these others are people of color from the (post)colonialized host country. Very occasionally producers picture white men with the models. These white men usually appear as athletes or sailors in the background of the picture, or as the sport-related companions of the models. Producers almost completely exclude white women other than the models, and with one exception they also exclude white children.

Thus, *Sports Illustrated* defines the cultural other as non-white. The other is not only culturally different from the self, but also racially different. Representing the cultural other as a person of color confirms the conclusion of the previous chapter—the hegemonic masculine subject, as expressed through *Sports Illustrated,* is white.

The swimsuit issue reinforces several racist notions about the Self and Other. It suggests that the recently decolonialized world is "black" and the United States (and Western world) is "white," obscuring the fact that many people of color live in the United States and many whites reside in the recently decolonialized world. It implies that people of color are (always) vastly culturally different from whites. Even more seriously, these representations link negative traits that are associated with the (post)colonialized world (which will be discussed below) with people of color, and thus insinuate that whites are generally superior to people of color.

### The Other Is Uncivilized, So the Self Is Civilized

One negative characteristic Westerners frequently attribute to people from (post)colonialized countries is that they are uncivilized. Westerners often stereotype people from these countries as childlike and primitive (e.g., Carby, 1982; Dorfman & Mattelart, 1975; Gupta, 1986; Jan Mohamed & Llyod, 1987). They imagine (post)colonialized countries as static societies that resemble Western societies from the distant past (e.g., Clifford, 1987; Corbey, 1988; MacCannell, 1976). People from (post)colonialized countries are commonly associated with romantic views of nature and the natural (e.g., Bulbeck, 1988; Desnoes, 1988; Dorfman & Mattelart, 1975). This set of beliefs can be traced back to the early colonial period, when it served as one of the central justifications for colonialism.

The swimsuit issues reflect this Western mythology, representing the cultures of the (post)colonialized world as primitive, simplistic, and static, and the people in this world as childlike and natural. Although visual elements of the swimsuit issue texts help to create this meaning, by picturing people from (post)colonialized countries engaged in childlike play, with minimal to no clothing, or surrounded by nature, it is the written texts in the issue that most strongly suggest this interpretation. For example, the text of the swimsuit spread in 1971 says that the Dominican Republic " . . . hasn't changed much since Columbus discovered it" (p. 30), a preposterous notion. The author of a text in the 1991 issue describes the Caicus Islands as " . . . first discovered by Columbus in 1492 and still barely discovered by developers" (p. 91). The authors of these texts sometimes portray sports played in the (post)colonialized countries as ancient, ritualistic, and barbaric (e.g., 1986; 1988). This portrayal matches the general trend of Western media producers to depict sport in the (post)colonialized world as exotic (Whannel, 1985).

When the representations featured in the swimsuit issues intimate or directly state that the (post)colonialized world is simplistic, primitive, and static, these representations imply that Western cultures, and therefore Westerners themselves, are complex, modern, and changing. When the swimsuit issue suggests that the (post)colonialized Other is uncivilized, it also insinuates that the ideal reader of *Sports Illustrated* and the swimsuit issue, the Western masculine Self, is civilized.

### The Other Is a Sexual Object, So the Self Is a Sexual Subject

Westerners tend to associate sexual licentiousness and lustfulness with lack of civilization and with the cultures of (post)colonialized countries. Western media producers often portray people from (post)colonialized countries as sexually permissive and sexually exotic (e.g., Graham-Brown, 1988; Omolade, 1983; Scott, 1989).

Since Western consumers often associate (post)colonialized countries with sexual exoticism, simply picturing the swimsuit issue models in these countries buttresses the notion that the models exude eroticism. Sometimes the swimsuits the models wear reflect an ethnic motif of the host culture, which facilitates the transfer of sexual meaning allied with the host culture to the models. The captions also sometimes encourage this transfer of meaning, as in the 1988 issue in which one caption describes the swimwear as helping the model play "harem girl" (p. 80).

The ways *Sports Illustrated* producers represent people from (post)colonialized countries in the swimsuit issue communicates particular meanings about sexuality. As already mentioned, it is common for producers of the swimsuit issue to picture pre-adolescent boys from the (post)colonialized shooting location nearby the model. Often these boys wear minimum, and in one case no, clothing. Yet, interestingly, producers rarely show these boys looking at the model or the camera. Producers also include scantily clothed men from (post)colonialized countries in the pictures, and these men are depicted in ways that make them appear totally oblivious to the presence of the model or camera. For example, a picture in the 1978 swimsuit issue features one of the models sitting on a boat close to a man who is working with fishing nets, yet the man seems unaware of the model's presence. He bends over his work, and a straw hat shields his face from the camera. The models, on the other hand, sometimes look at the boys or men in the pictures.

Perhaps producers intend to signify the sexual licentiousness and exoticism of the (post)colonialized natives through the lack of clothing on the boys and men. These pictures probably work to reinforce the racist stereotype that people of color from (post)colonialized areas are sexually exotic and uninhibited. Yet, representing (post)colonialized natives as uninterested in the models or viewers may convey the point that the (post)colonialized natives are sexually innocent, a meaning that counters the notion that the (post)colonialized other is sexually ravenous and free from sexual inhibitions. This symbolic disregard also may relieve readers schooled in the racist taboo about interracial sexuality. The lack of attention to the models and readers also reserves the sexual gaze for *Sports Illustrated* readers.

It is clear that consumers of the swimsuit issue have been offered the position of sexual subject, as they have the opportunity to scrutinize pictures that highlight the bodies of both the (barely-dressed) models and people from (post)colonialized countries. The models serve as potential sexual objects for these consumers. Although the models usually look at the camera/audience, these looks are shaped to signify subservience and thus invite the audience gaze rather than challenge it. But the models occasionally act as (sexual) subjects in the pictures when they look at the people from the (post)colonialized countries who appear in the pictures with them. Thus, white Western women, as represented by the models in the magazine, mainly serve as sexual objects of the masculine gaze, but possess some agency when they are permitted to gaze at people of color from the (post)colonialized world. People of color from the (post)colonialized world, who do not look at anyone, serve as "exotic" objects for (white) Western visual inspection. The white Western masculine self, the ideal reader of *Sports Illustrated* and the swimsuit issue, is the supreme sexual subject who can gaze at all others.

### *The Other Serves Me, So I Am a Member of the Leisure Class*

In *Sports Illustrated*, people from the (post)colonialized countries not only serve as exotic objects for the tourist's examination, but they also literally serve the tourists. The swimsuit issue portrays people from (post)colonialized countries as members of the service class.

As already mentioned, when people from (post)colonialized countries are pictured nearby the models, they often (seem to) serve or entertain the model, or they are independently engaged in work. The model, contrarily, is usually not participating in work or service, and thus clearly represents the arena of leisure.

The written texts in the swimsuit issues also commonly depict people from (post)colonialized countries as performing services for Western visitors. Such services include the roles of guides, physical laborers, "exotic performers," and waiters. In the 1989 swimsuit issue, for example, the author of one article portrays the people from Mexico as strange caddies, inarticulate housekeepers, and exotic entertainers for vacationers.

People from (post)colonialized countries are represented by the authors of these written texts as ideally suited for, and enjoying, their service roles. The people from (post)colonialized countries are often described as friendly, trustworthy, and polite. For example, in the 1986 issue, a caption says, "While watching a dance group do its stuff at the Hotel Bora Bora, Elle, whose swimsuit is by Gideon Oberson ($54), discovers that even the littlest natives are friendly" (p. 133).

The swimsuit issues suggest that consumers should regard people from (post)colonialized countries as existing chiefly for the sole purpose of providing services for white Western vacationers. These texts reinforce the belief that people who live in these countries have a natural inclination for labor that involves heavy physical exertion, "exotic" entertainment, and serving other people. Conversely, it is implied that Westerners are tourists who deserve to be served by these (post)-colonialized others.

By defining its readers as Western tourists who are served by other people, and by intimating that its readers possess a playful attitude and enjoy activities associated with leisure, *Sports Illustrated* characterizes its readers as members of the leisure class. Thus, the hegemonic masculine subject, as exemplified by *Sports Illustrated* and its swimsuit issue, is at least an honorary member of the leisure class.

Members of the Western leisure class have a history of exploiting others. The notions that people from the (post)colonialized world are ideal laborers, who should be below Westerners in the economic hierarchy and supply services for their Western superiors, have roots in colonial history and provide ideological support for the continued exploitation of labor from (post)colonialized countries. Earlier, through the system of slavery, many Westerners did not pay anything for this labor. Now Western businesspeople flock to the (post)colonialized world so that they can increase their profits by paying rock-bottom wages. Tourism is an element of this story, as Westerners travel to parts of the (post)colonialized world for the inexpensive services, entertainment, and material goods available from the "exotic" local residents. Increasingly, there is a global division of labor, where people from the so-called core countries (i.e., the wealthy countries, comprised of most of the Western world and Japan) control the majority of the world's resources and many can pay for the goods and services they need and want, while people from the so-called peripheral countries (i.e., the poor countries, comprised of most of the previously colonialized countries in Africa, South America, Central America, the West Indies, and Asia) produce goods for businesspeople from the core countries for meager wages. The way that the swimsuit issue represents the (post)colonialized world and the relationship of this world to the Western world, reinforces this exploitative worldwide division of labor.

## The Other Is Feminine and Inferior, So the Self Is Masculine and Superior

Many of the ways that the (post)colonialized world is depicted coincide with characteristics allied with hegemonic femininity. Like people from the (post)colonialized world, feminine women are seen as culturally different (from men), childlike, close to nature, sexual objects, and best suited for roles that involve service to other people. In other words, the (post)colonialized world is associated with femininity. The Western world, contrarily, is deemed masculine, as it is linked with more masculine characteristics.

Of course, the (post)colonialized world is not simply portrayed as different from the West, but also inferior. In contemporary United States society, being conceived of as feminine, a person of color, a sexual object, uncivilized, and a member of the social class that serves others is associated with inferiority. Inversely, being thought of as masculine, white, a sexual subject, civilized, and a member of the social class that is served by others is allied with superiority.

When an association between the (post)colonialized world and inferiority becomes part of our cultural common sense, continued dominance of the (post)colonialized world by the West is easily justified. The swimsuit issue is one text among many that reinforces this commonsense association, and thus it contributes to the context that legitimates Western dominance.

Because the hegemonic masculine ideal embraces Western identity, the status of this ideal is enhanced by the association with Western culture. In its extreme, the hegemonic masculine subject is not only seen as superior, but is the actual colonizer of others.

### *The Hegemonic Masculine Subject as Colonizer of "the (Post)Colonialized Other"*

The wealth accumulated during the colonial period of capitalism was built on the backs of people from the colonialized countries, as these people served as a pool of inexpensive labor and their lands were used as a source of cheap resources. Today, in the multinational period of capitalism, Western countries continue to build their wealth on the backs of people from the (post)colonialized countries through the same mechanisms of exploiting labor and natural resources. These international relations of dominance and exploitation have devastated the economies of most countries in the (post)colonialized world, and poverty reigns in these regions. Most attempts to reduce the poverty in these countries have been unsuccessful as they have not addressed the root causes of the poverty. Also, such efforts often result in major debt to Western investors. This contemporary Western material dominance over (post)colonialized countries is accompanied by symbolic colonialism.

*The Nature of Contemporary Symbolic Colonialism*

Symbolic colonialism by tourists resembles the colonialism of the past in three respects. First, colonizers during both periods claim that they have "discovered" new lands and/or people. In the past the colonizers literally discovered land and peoples that they did not know about previously, whereas symbolic colonialism involves the discovery of attractive tourist destinations. An "attractive tourist destination" contains natural and human phenomena that the tourist has never seen before, and can therefore "discover." "Attractive tourist destinations" are also those places that offer the comforts desired by Westerners and yet are not "overrun" by other tourists; for how can one "discover" a place that so many other people have already "discovered"?

Second, both bygone colonialism and symbolic colonialism are justified through discourse that maintains that the (post)colonialized regions are uninhabited or uncivilized. In the past, colonizers thought it was okay to occupy land if nobody else was believed to reside there, or if the people who lived there were considered so inferior that they needed "guidance" from the colonizers. Today, tourists are drawn to places that they think are uninhabited or sparsely inhabited, and to places where the people are regarded as less civilized than (and thus very different from) the tourists.

Third, colonizers during both periods "capture" people and lands. During past colonialism, the colonizers literally captured the land and/or people of a region, while during the contemporary period of symbolic colonialism the tourist "captures" this land and people in photographs (van den Berghe & Keyes, 1984; Williamson, 1986). Some scholars argue that "photograph hunting" in (post)colonialized countries has replaced real hunting (e.g., Graham-Brown, 1988; Haraway, 1984/85; Sontag, 1978). Tourists often desire to possess symbols of ethnicity from the countries they visit (Graburn, 1984; MacCannell, 1976; 1984), and photographs suit this purpose well. These photographs serve as proof to other Westerners that the tourist truly "discovered" this land/people.

The swimsuit issue texts both reflect and reinforce a colonialist mentality. These texts often glorify past colonialism by celebrating a distorted and idealized version of the history of relationships between Western countries and colonialized countries. For example, several times the authors of the texts state that Columbus "discovered" the locations that appear in the photographs (1971; 1983; 1991). And the author of a 1986 swimsuit issue article about Tahitian sport implies that Tahiti was primitive before Europeans arrived.

The (post)colonialized settings for the swimsuit issue shoots are not simply represented as sites of the glorious colonial past, but also as places that are open to future symbolic colonialism by tourists. For example, the author of the written text accompanying the 1971 swimsuit spread says that the Dominican Republic is "a lost paradise regained" (p. 30), implying that this region has been "regained," or re-colonialized, by tourists.

The notions that (post)colonialized lands are available for discovery by tourists, and that tourists should travel to these lands to experience uninhabited and uncivilized paradise, are commonly suggested in the swimsuit issues. For example, the written text appearing in the 1990 spread claims that the Windward Islands remain "Unspoiled. Unexpected. All but undiscovered" (p. 99). A 1989 swimsuit issue article that encourages readers to travel to Mexico states, "Hurry, our precivilization sale ends soon" (p. 272).

The theme of the tourist capturing the (post)colonialized world through photographs is embodied in the swimsuit issue pictures themselves. The producers of the swimsuit issue are literally tourists in the lands they photograph, and their photographs do "capture" what are regarded as the "exotic" features of the lands and societies they visit. *Sports Illustrated* readers, through viewing these swimsuit issue photographs, become media tourists of these lands.

## Problems with Symbolic Colonialism

Some argue that the tourist industry will bring about salvation for (post)colonialized countries, but the history of relations between colonizers and colonized should move us to suspect this judgment. Tourism in (post)colonialized countries entails a dependence on Western countries, as most of the tourists come from the West. And the industry of tourism involves much economic, cultural, and environmental exploitation in the host countries. Urry (1990), who has written at length about this matter, notes that:

> Much tourist investment in the developing world has in fact been undertaken by large-scale companies based in North America and Western Europe, and the bulk of such tourist expenditure is retained by the transnational companies involved: only 2–25 percent of the retail price remains in the host country. (p. 64)

In many host countries, the wealth from tourism does not trickle-down to the masses, and many tourist facilities provide few benefits for the indigenous population. When tourism accounts for an extremely high percentage of the national income, anything that reduces the amount of tourism in the country has economically-disastrous consequences (Urry, 1990). Finally, much of the employment indigenous people obtain in the tourist industry requires little skill, involves little mental input and self-determination, and results in low pay. It thus "may well reproduce the servile character of the previous colonial regime . . ." (Urry, 1990, pp. 64–65).

The discourse that advertises tourism in (post)colonialized countries is a problem, as well. The notions that the (post)colonialized lands are "undiscovered" and "untouched" are as offensive today as they were in the past, because the people who live in these countries have been "touching" their places of residence for a long time, and the notion of "discovery" implies that these inhabitants do not count as human.

As previously discussed, both actual and mediated tourism involve the consumption of cultural difference. Of course, there is nothing wrong with learning about other cultures. Unquestionably, differences exist between people whose lives have been shaped by different cultures and structural circumstances, and achieving an understanding of different cultures and structural circumstances can foster peace and cooperation among people throughout the world. Yet, in much Western discourse, including the discourse associated with tourism, cultural differences are represented in oversimplified and misleading ways because this discourse reflects dichotomous and hierarchical thinking. Like the colonialism of old, the symbolic colonizer usually views the other not just as different, but as inferior. Thus, much of the contemporary discourse related to tourism bolsters continued Western material dominance over the (post)colonialized world.

The discourse surrounding the practices of tourism is also deleterious because it obscures problems at the (post)colonialized tourist sites. Although most citizens of Western countries seem somewhat aware of the wretched poverty that prevails in (post)colonialized countries, they appear to be unaware of the factors that generated and perpetuate this poverty. The mainstream media, for the most part, contributes to Western ignorance, as the poverty is either ignored altogether or represented in ways that conceal its causes. Many times no reasons are expressed for the poverty, while other times the explanations described are simplistic and/or misleading (Gupta, 1986; Hart, 1989). In some media texts, (post)colonialized lands are portrayed as poverty stricken regions of social chaos (e.g., Gupta, 1986; Desnoes, 1985; Thomas &

Bernstein, 1985). In other media texts, including the texts that focus on tourism, producers depict (post)colonialized countries as idealized lands of unpolluted jungle and beach paradise without any problems (e.g., Desnoes, 1985; 1988; Chapkis, 1986).

The swimsuit issues must be understood in the context of the poverty that dominates many of the countries where the pictures are shot. The swimsuit issue texts represent (post)colonialized countries as utopian tropical lands for vacation, while ignoring the real economic conditions in these countries and the colonial histories that largely created these conditions. Why does *Sports Illustrated* fail to portray the poverty in these countries? A central reason must be the connection between the swimsuit issue and Western tourism. Most actual and media tourists will not enjoy themselves in an atmosphere where desolate poverty is constantly evident. Certainly, if *Sports Illustrated* offered accurate and comprehensive details of colonial history and poverty, many consumers from the United States would feel so uncomfortable that they would cease consumption of the swimsuit issue and perhaps of other components of tourism as well. Obviously, this is a case where economic motives overwhelm social concerns. Clearly, Time Incorporated (the owner of *Sports Illustrated*) is not the only company driven by this economic imperative, as the tourist industry itself is moved by capitalistic goals. Yet, in contributing to the mass media practice of obscuring the existence and origins of (post)colonial poverty, *Sports Illustrated* producers do nothing to raise the consciousness that is necessary to reverse the economic exploitation that generates this poverty.

## The Hegemonic Masculine Subject as Symbolic Colonizer

Contemporary hegemonic masculinity has its roots in an earlier form of hegemonic masculinity from the colonial period (Connell, 1995). In the colonial past, one of the most common symbols of hegemonic masculinity was the colonizer. Famous and admired men included colonizers like Cecil Rhodes, who was instrumental in expanding the British empire in Africa. Contemporary hegemonic masculinity even retains a flavor of past colonialism. For example, a popular icon of contemporary hegemonic masculinity is the cowboy, a symbol of prior colonialism in the United States.

Although not a fan of Freudian analysis, and thus not fully persuaded by all of the arguments made by Paul Hoch (1979), I am convinced of Hoch's contentions that colonialism was partly driven by the desire to prove one's manhood and that contemporary masculinity continues to be achieved by "white heroes" who dominate "black beasts." By "black beasts," Hoch not only means people of color, but also other nations, the feminine elements of the male self, and a man's own homosexual tendencies. Hoch maintains that patriotism is "almost the secular religion of an assertion of collective manhood," and nationalism "becomes combative masculinity raised to the communal level" (p. 116).

Sports Illustrated and its swimsuit issue reflect and reinforce a model of contemporary hegemonic masculinity that is allied with a contemporary version of colonialism, symbolic colonialism. The hegemonic masculine subject is a symbolic colonizer, an actual and media tourist, who views "the (post)colonialized other" as exotic spectacle. The hegemonic masculine subject believes that people from (post)colonialized lands are inferior because they are culturally and sexually exotic, uncivilized, and feminized people of color who have a natural inclination for serving other people. Contrarily, the hegemonic masculine subject regards himself as culturally, racially, and sexually superior, and deserving of a superior economic position. Hegemonic masculinity, exemplified in Sports Illustrated's swimsuit issue, is built on the backs of the (post)colonialized other, meaning that this form of masculinity justifies ideas and practices that debilitate indigenous people from the (post)colonialized world.

# *Conclusion*

Although the social context shapes audience perspectives, and these perspectives affect audience interpretations of media texts, it is clear that production processes and textual content greatly influence the creation of cultural meaning. Just because media texts do not directly determine the thoughts and behaviors of consumers does not mean that these texts are irrelevant. Media texts do mold consumer interpretations, and they contribute to an atmosphere of discourse that indirectly shapes consumer thoughts and actions.

Although consumers decode the swimsuit issue in a variety of ways, and thus this text serves as a stimulus for a struggle over meaning, the producers of the issue set the stage for this struggle. The combination of textual suggestions of meaning and our own cultural knowledge regarding the symbols used by producers, leads most of us to create common accounts of the content and ideal readers of the swimsuit issue. Thereafter the conflict over meaning ensues, but the topics of the conflict, gender and sexuality, do not seem very negotiable for consumers immersed in United States culture.

*Sports Illustrated* producers attempt to increase their profit by fashioning *Sports Illustrated* to be a magazine about hegemonic masculinity rather than a sports magazine. The swimsuit issue and a narrow definition of sport help them to accomplish this goal. *Sports Illustrated* producers have achieved success with this strategy, since the magazine attracts a huge audience of men and reaps enormous profits. One reason why *Sports Illustrated* and its swimsuit issue are so popular with so many men is that the gender order, and thus hegemonic masculinity, have been under attack by feminists in recent years. Men who support the current gender order can use *Sports Illustrated* to celebrate hegemonic masculinity in the face of these challenges. The popularity of the swimsuit spread is also enhanced by its appearance in a sports magazine, which contributes to its acceptance in many public settings. This moves many boys/men to choose the swimsuit issue, rather than less acceptable forms of sexual representation, in their efforts to secure masculine status and resist sexual repression.

Textual content and structure not only influence consumer interpretations, but also affect the amount of pleasure consumers can derive from particular texts. Those who create preferred readings of media texts often attain more pleasure from these texts than those who create oppositional readings. This is because textual structure and content tend to affirm the identities and beliefs of those who create preferred readings.

People who enjoy the swimsuit issue usually hold conservative opinions about gender and attempt to conform to hegemonic masculine and feminine ideals. The swimsuit issue pleases these readers, because it supports their conservative beliefs and gender identities. Those who dislike the swimsuit issue for the most part hold either reactionary views of sexuality or feminist convictions. The swimsuit issue texts distress them, rather than provide pleasure, because the content and structure of these texts conflict with their beliefs and desired sense of self. Men (and the much smaller number of women) who appreciate the swimsuit issue are considerably more likely to purchase and read, and enjoy the controversy surrounding, the swimsuit issue than people who create oppositional readings. People who criticize the swimsuit issue usually do not purchase it, read it regularly, or enjoy participating in the debate about it. Rather, many people who dislike the swimsuit issue display their lack of pleasure by never subscribing, or cancelling their subscription, to *Sports Illustrated*.

Because media texts influence reader interpretations, and the amount of pleasure readers can derive through consumption, it is necessary for scholars to furnish critical commentary on mainstream media texts. In particular, scholars should articulate public critiques of those media texts that help to reinforce inequality and those texts that offer less pleasure for the least powerful categories of people and their supporters. Consumers should also be encouraged to contribute to this project, by creating oppositional readings that address issues of inequality relative to these texts.

Consumers do express varied oppositional readings of the swimsuit issue. The issue functions as a catalyst for a national debate about hegemonic masculinity and hegemonic femininity. Consumers' interpretations of the swimsuit issue are shaped by their divergent views about gender and sexuality, views which have been molded by their specific social experiences. Consumers clash over the morality of representations which signify sexual meaning. They differ over whether heterosexuality should be regarded as an essential component of masculinity. They quarrel over whether sport should be narrowly defined as elite men's spectator sport, or such definitions should be expanded to include equal coverage of women's sport. Consumers debate whether women should be viewed primarily in terms of their appearance and sexual appeal, or seen as whole persons.

Many readings of the swimsuit issue exhibit resistance to the current gender order. But as Budd, Entman and Steinman (1990) warn, we should not make too much of oppositional readings, because the mere existence of these readings does not inevitably result in social change. Also, people who create these readings are not necessarily engaged in activism that helps to produce social change.

Verbal and written criticisms of *Sports Illustrated* do not directly influence the amount of power women possess in United States society. Such criticisms have not even affected *Sports Illustrated* itself, as it continues to publish the swimsuit issue and feature unequal coverage of women's and men's sport.

To generate social change, it is necessary to move beyond criticizing the media texts that currently exist. We need to attempt to influence media production processes, so that the arena of popular culture will offer more texts that affirm the identities and beliefs of people who are presently dedicated to eradicating current forms of injustice, and help to transform the beliefs of people who have not yet acquired such a commitment.

Some scholars, activists, and organizations concerned about bias in the sport media have begun to target media producers. The Women's Sports Foundation (1995) and Canadian Association for the Advancement of Women and Sports and Physical Activity (1990s) produce and distribute guidelines designed to help media producers, women athletes, and others detect sexism in and purge sexism from the media coverage of women athletes. The Women's Sports Foundation tried to get the Atlanta Committee for the 1996 Olympic Games to eliminate gender bias from the proposed pictograms for these Games (Chroni, Bunker & Sabo, 1995). The Amateur Athletic Foundation of Los Angeles not only sponsors studies about bias in the sports media (Duncan, Messner, Jensen & Wachs, 1994; Duncan, Messner & Williams, 1991; Duncan, Messner, Williams & Jensen, 1990; Sabo et al., 1996), but also endeavors to educate media producers about this bias by hosting conferences, by writing press releases and holding press conferences that report the results of these studies, and by giving copies of these studies directly to media producers and to journalism/communication studies departments at universities (Wilson, W., 1996). For almost a decade, on the day the swimsuit issue first appeared in the newsstands, the organizations Women Against Pornography and Men Against Pornography have protested at the Time-Life Building (Smith, L. W., 1996).

Affecting the media production process is a difficult task, because most mass media producers are motivated by the pursuit of profit from advertisers. These profits are obtained by securing the target audiences that advertisers desire. Despite this, some interest groups do influence the media production process, more so if they exhort the advertisers instead of the media producers themselves (Turow, 1984).

During the early 1990s, Linnea Smith (see Appendix B) initiated a campaign against the *Sports Illustrated* swimsuit issue that addressed companies that advertise in the swimsuit issue. For sixteen dollars, Smith offered a "protest package" that consisted of professionally designed postcards, address labels for the swimsuit issue advertisers, sample protest letters, and information booklets for use in a letter writing campaign. She also distributed stickers and buttons as part of her drive. Today, Smith works with the organizations Media Action Alliance and Media Watch. Every year these organizations ask their newsletter subscribers to send protest letters to the swimsuit issue advertisers and the organizations provide the addresses of these advertisers to facilitate the letter writing campaigns (Smith, L. W., 1996).

It seems particularly difficult to change texts that signify hegemonic masculinity, as many of these texts attract a large audience of affluent men, an audience desirable to numerous advertisers. It appears that *Sports Illustrated* will not submit to feminist demands that the magazine eliminate (or substantially change) the swimsuit issue, and cover men's and women's sport in an equitable way, because profits from advertisers would decrease. Shaping *Sports Illustrated* into solely a sports magazine, rather than a men's magazine, simply is not a profitable strategy.

The problem with *Sports Illustrated*'s practice of securing a large audience of men by creating an atmosphere of hegemonic masculinity is that on the way to the bank it tramples over women, gays/lesbians, people of color, and people from the (post)colonialized world. Hegemonic masculinity itself is defined as the antithesis of these others, and thus is built on the backs of these others. The hegemonic masculine ideal is sexist because it defines women primarily in terms of their sexual/beauty appeal to men, and men with respect to their power over other people. The ideal is heterosexist, because it encourages the belief that heterosexuality is superior to homosexuality/bisexuality, and that "real men" are heterosexual. Hegemonic masculinity is racist because it characterizes people of color as vastly different from and inferior to whites. And finally, the hegemonic masculine ideal is ethnocentric because it is built upon the notion that people from the (post)colonialized world are inferior, and should be subordinate, to Westerners. By reinforcing these prejudiced beliefs, *Sports Illustrated* encourages individual and institutional practices that produce and maintain these forms of inequality.

Some people argue that we need new ideals of masculinity and femininity, and that these new forms of gender will help to subvert gender, racial, ethnic, and sexual inequality. Yet, the very existence of masculine and feminine ideals accentuates gender differences, and history has demonstrated that such differences usually serve the cause of gender inequality. Thus, what we really need to do is abolish the gender ideals of masculinity and femininity altogether.

This implies that media texts should be shaped in ways that obscure and contradict (present conceptions of) gender difference. For example, sexual representations could include people of all genders, races, and ethnicities, and people who by their appearance challenge gender stereotypes and the gender categories themselves. Mixed messages ought to be given in regard to the ideal subject position of these texts. Texts about sport could feature equal or more coverage of women, and more types and levels of sport participation. If *Sports Illustrated* made these sorts of changes, it might lose profits, but it would serve the cause of justice and be a magazine for all.

# Sports Illustrated's
# Swimsuit Issues
# (from 1964 to 1991 and 1996)

*January 20, 1964*
  First official swimsuit issue
        Location: Caribbean
        Photographer: J. Frederick Smith
        Cover Model: Babette March
*January 18, 1965*
        Location: Baja, California
        Photographer: Jay Maisel
        Cover Model: Sue Peterson
*January 17, 1966*
        Location: Bahamas, West Indies
        Photographer: Howell Conant
        Cover Model: Sunny Bippus
*January 16, 1967*
        Location: Arizona
        Photographer: Jay Maisel
        Cover Model: Marilyn Tindall
*January 15, 1968*
        Location: Bora Bora Islands, South Pacific Islands
        Photographer: John Zimmerman
        Cover Model: Turia Mau
*January 13, 1969*
        Location: Puerto Rico, West Indies
        Photographer: Ernie Haas
        Cover Model: Jamee Becker

*January 12, 1970*
    Location: Hawaii, Central Pacific Islands
    Photographer: Jay Maisel
    Cover Model: Cheryl Tiegs
*February 1, 1971*
    Location: Dominican Republic, West Indies
    Photographer: Robert Huntzinger
    Cover Model: Tannia Rubiano
*January 17, 1972*
    Location: Los Angeles, California coast area
    Photographer: John Zimmerman
    Cover Model: Shelia Roscoe
*January 29, 1973*
    Location: Caribbean
    Photographer: Walter Iooss, Jr.
    Cover Model: Dayle Haddon
*January 28, 1974*
    Location: Puerto Rico, West Indies
    Photographer: Jay Maisel
    Cover Model: Ann Simonton
*January 27, 1975*
    Location: Cancun, Mexico
    Photographer: Walter Iooss, Jr.
    Cover Model: Cheryl Tiegs
*January 19, 1976*
    Location: Baja, California
    Photographer: Kourken Pakchanian
    Cover Models: Yvette and Yvonne Sylvander (twins)
*January 24, 1977*
    Location: Maui, Hawaii, Central Pacific Islands
    Photographer: Art Kane
    Cover Model: Lena Kansbod
*January 16, 1978*
    Location: Brazil
    Photographer: Walter Iooss, Jr.
    Cover Model: Maria Joao
*February 5, 1979*
    Location: Seychelles, West Indies
    Photographer: Walter Iooss, Jr.
    Cover Model: Christie Brinkley

*February 4, 1980*
    Location: British Virgin Islands, West Indies
    Photographer: John Zimmerman
    Cover Model: Christie Brinkley
*February 9, 1981*
    Location: Florida
    Photographer: John Zimmerman
    Cover Model: Christie Brinkley
*February 8, 1982*
    Location: Kenya
    Photographer: John Zimmerman
    Cover Model: Carol Alt
*February 14, 1983*
    Location: Jamaica, West Indies
    Photographer: Walter Iooss, Jr.
    Cover Model: Cheryl Tiegs
*February 13, 1984*
    Location: Aruba, West Indies
    Photographer: Paolo Curto
    Cover Model: Paulina Porizkova
*February 11, 1985*
    Location: Australia
    Photographer: Brian Lanker
    Cover Model: Paulina Porizkova
*February 10, 1986*
    Location: Bora Bora Islands, South Pacific Islands
    Photographer: Brian Lanker
    Cover Model: Elle MacPherson
*February 9, 1987*
    Location: Dominican Republic, West Indies
    Photographer: John Zimmerman
    Cover Model: Elle MacPherson
*February 15, 1988*
    Location: Thailand
    Photographer: Marc Hispard
    Cover Model: Elle MacPherson
*February, 1989*
    Special 25th Anniversary Swimsuit Issue
    Locations: Mexico, Seychelles (West Indies), Utah, Florida, Kenya,
        Kauai (Hawaii, Central Pacific Islands), St. Barthelemy (Carib-
        bean), and Australia

Photographers: Paolo Curto, Robert Huntzinger, John Zimmerman, Walter Iooss, Jr., Marc Hispard, and Jay Maisel

Cover Models: Kathy Ireland, Cheryl Tiegs, Yvette and Yvonne Sylvander, Christie Brinkley, Carol Alt, Paulina Porizkova, and Elle MacPherson

*February 12, 1990*

Location: Grenadines, West Indies

Photographer: Robert Huntzinger

Cover Model: Judit Masco

*February 11, 1991*

Locations: Club Med Cruise Lines in Caribbean, Spice Islander Cruise Lines in Indonesia, and Caicos Sol Charter in Caicos Islands, West Indies

Photographers: Walter Iooss, Jr., Marc Hispard, and Hans Feurer

Cover Model: Ashley Montana

*January 29, 1996*

Location: South Africa

Photographers: Walter Iooss, Jr., Robert Huntzinger, and Marco Glaviano

Cover Models: Valeria Mazzo and Tyra Banks

# Appendix B

## Non-Academic Media Material Related to the Swimsuit Issues

### Calendars and Diaries

1989 *Sports Illustrated* Swimsuit Calendar. (1988). Time, Inc. Photographer Marc Hispard. Senior Editor Jule Campbell.

1990 *Sports Illustrated* Swimsuit Calendar. (1989). Time, Inc. Photographers Marc Hispard, Paolo Curto, Walter Iooss. Jr., & Jay Maisel. Senior Editor Jule Campbell.

1990 *Sports Illustrated* 25th Swimsuit Anniversary Diary. (1989). Time, Inc. Senior Editor Jule Campbell.

1991 *Sports Illustrated* Swimsuit Calendar. (1990). Time, Inc. Photographer Robert Huntzinger. Senior Editor Jule Campbell.

1991 *Sports Illustrated* Swimsuit Diary. (1990). Time, Inc. Senior Editor Jule Campbell.

### Miscellaneous Materials

A. G. & C. Productions. "*Sports Illustrated* Swimsuit Competition . . ." [Birthday Card.] Chicago, IL: Recycled Paper Products, Inc.

Mailed Advertisement for 1990 *Sports Illustrated* Swimsuit Issue Calendar and Diary.

Mailed Advertisement for 1991 *Sports Illustrated* Sweepstake Contest.

Mailed Advertisement for 1991 *Sports Illustrated* Swimsuit Issue Calendar and Diary.

Mailed Advertisement for 1992 *Sports Illustrated* Swimsuit Issue Calendar and Diary.

Simonton, A. (1989, July 6). *Oral Presentation.* Univ. of Iowa.

Smith, L. W. (1990s). [Various postcards, booklets, lists of advertiser addresses, sample letters, stickers, and buttons that are part of "protest packages" designed to enable people to work against the *Sports Illustrated* swimsuit issue.] Chapel Hill, NC: Linnea Smith.

*The Sports Illustrated Catalog.* (1990, Fall).

"This is the Birthday Card You've Been Waiting for . . ." [Birthday Card.] Chicago, IL: Recycled Paper Products.

### Newspaper and Magazine Material

Adler, J., Darnton, N., & Barrett, T. (1989, Feb. 13). The Fanciest Dive: A Midwinter Whim Becomes a $30 Million Bonanza. *Newsweek:* 53–54.

Barreiro, D. (1989, Feb. 10). No Coverup for this Debate. *Star Tribune:* 1C & 5C.

Barreiro, D. (1989, Feb. 20). *SI's* Swimsuits Get No Support. *Star Tribune:* 1C & 7C.

Bentley, R. (1991, August 19). Her Doll is Built Like Real Women. *Star Tribune:* 1E & 7E.

Coleman, N. (1989, Feb. 12). Magazine Annually Brings Out Boy in All of Us. *St. Paul Pioneer Press Dispatch:* 3B.

DeMont, J. (1989, Feb. 20). Tapping a Market: Swimsuit Magazines are Earning Big Profits. *Macleans, 102* (8): 28.

Donaton, S., & Winters, P. (1990, April 9). Diet Pepsi Teams Up With *"SI"*. *Advertising Age, 61*(15): 55.

Elliott, S. (1989, Feb. 6). The Magazine is a Market of Its Own. *USA Today:* 4D.

Johnson, R. G. (1989, March 5). Swimsuit Pose Sins of Flesh. *The Commercial Appeal* (Memphis).

Jule, T. (1990, June). Swimsuit Issue Protests. *Off Our Backs, 20*(6): 27.

Koelln, G. (1989, March 19). The Tide Turns. *St.Paul Pioneer Press Dispatch:* 8K.

Lieberman D. (1989, Jan. 16). *SI's* Swimsuit Issue: More than Meets the Eye. *Business Week, 3087:* 52.

Peterson, K. S. (1989, Feb. 6). On the Anniversary Cover a Glimpse of Ireland. *USA Today:* 4D.

Reilly, P. (1988, Oct. 17). "Sport" Now Ready to Tackle *"SI"*. *Advertising Age, 59*(44): 37.

Robinson, K. (1991, Feb. 15). Making It. [Cartoon.] *Chicago Tribune:* Sec. 7.

Rubarth, L. D. (1990, Jan./Feb.). An Ironic Celebration. *Women & Sport,* *3*(1): 2.

Rubarth, L. D. (1990, Jan./Feb.). Nike Knows Exploitation. *Women and Sports 3*(1): 2.

Sage, D. (1989, Spring). [Letter to Editor.] *Media Watch, 3*(1): 8.

Staff. (1989, Feb. 28). Jockbeat. *The Village Voice:* 130

Staff. (1989, March 11). Reiko Says Suits are Sexy, But Feminine. *Star Tribune:* 10E.

Staff. (1989, Spring). Women in Sports. *Media Watch, 3*(1): 5.

Staff. (1989, Summer). Exploiting Women in Sports Magazines. *Challenging Media Images of Women, 1*(3).

Trudeau, G. (1989, Jan. 23, 24, 25, 26, 27 & 28). Doonesbury. [Cartoon.] *Star Tribune:* Sec. E.

## Swimsuit Issues Produced by Other Magazines

*Ebony Man.* (1991, Jan.). Vol. *6*(2).

*Spin.* (1989, July). Vol. *5*(4).

*Sport.* (1991, Feb.).

## Audiovisual Materials

*Current Affair.* [Television Program.] (1988, Jan. 17).

*Elle MacPherson's International Swimsuit 1991.* [Television Program.] (1991, May 17).

*Entertainment Tonight.* [Television Program.] (1990, Nov. 14).

*Entertainment Tonight.* [Television Program.] (1991, Feb. 6).

*Inside Edition.* [Television Program.] (1992, March 3).

*International Swimsuit Edition.* [Television Program.] (1989, July 23).

*Keystone Beer commercial.* [Television Advertisement.]

*NFL Clothing Commercial.* [Television Advertisement.] (1990, Dec. 2).

*Sports Illustrated 25th Anniversary Swimsuit Video.* (1989). Time, Inc.

*Swimsuit.* [Television Movie.] NBC.

*Yogurt Commercial.* [Television Advertisement.] (1991, May).

# Appendix C

## Interview Schedules for Producers, Consumers, and Librarians

### Interview Schedule for Producers

Although questions varied depending on the production role of the interview subject, as well as the flow of the conversation, some of the basic questions included:

1) What is your role in the making of the swimsuit issue?
2) How much and what type of control do you have over the product?
3) How has your work impacted the product?
4) Who is your boss and who works under you, and how does this system work?
5) Do you think the swimsuit issue has changed much over the years? If so, how has it changed?
6) What does the swimsuit issue mean to you? Has this meaning changed for you over time? If so, how has the meaning changed for you?
7) What do you think the swimsuit means to others?
8) When constructing the swimsuit issue, what do you think is looked for in a model? Why? What do you think is looked for in a picture setting? Why? What do you think is looked for in a photographer? Why? What do you think is looked for in the pictures that are selected for publication? Why?
9) What do you think the relationship is between *Sports Illustrated,* sports, and the swimsuit issue? (If they did

not understand this question, I asked the following: Do you think that sport and the swimsuit spread fit together? Why do you think that the swimsuit spread is published in *Sports Illustrated?*)

10) What do you think the relationship is between the swimsuit issue and swimsuits or the selling of these suits?

Of course, given the specific nature of some of the production roles, not all of these questions had relevance for all of the interviewed producers. I asked some of the interviewed producers questions that specifically apply to their roles in the production process.

## Interview Schedule for Librarians

In general, I asked the library workers the following questions:

1) What does your library typically do with *Sports Illustrated* to provide public access to it?

2) Do you use this same procedure for the swimsuit issue? If yes—Do you have any problem doing this? Please explain if there are any problems. If no—What do you do differently with the swimsuit issue? Please explain.

3) Is there anything else you can tell me about the swimsuit issue in relation to your library?

## Interview Schedule for Consumers

In general, I asked the interviewed consumers the following questions:

1) What magazines do you read regularly?

2) Do you watch sport regularly on television? Listen on the radio? Read about it in the paper? Read about it in magazines? Watch it live?

3) Do you read *Sports Illustrated* magazine regularly?

4) Do you read or look at the *Sports Illustrated* swimsuit issue? If no—Why not? If yes—Why do you read the swimsuit issue? Describe the manner in which you read the issue. What do you do with the swimsuit issue during the period when you are reading it? What do you do with the swimsuit issue after you are done reading it?

5) What does the swimsuit issue mean to you?

6) Has your opinion of the swimsuit issue changed over time? If yes, how so?

7) What do you think the swimsuit issue means to others?

8) Why do you think the people at *Sports Illustrated* publish this issue?

9) What do you think the relationship is between the swimsuit issue and sports?

10) What do you think the relationship is between the swimsuit issue and swimsuit fashion?

11) What is your age? Race or ethnic group? Sex? Occupation, if any? Sport participation?

12) Is your total yearly household income under 25,000 dollars, between 25,000 and 40,000 dollars, between 40,000 and 70,000 dollars, between 70,000 and 100,000 dollars, or over 100,000 dollars?

# Appendix D

# Recruitment of, and Information about, the Interviewed Producers and Consumers

## Recruitment of, and Information about, Interviewed Producers

I identified and contacted the interviewed producers with the help of information from *Sports Illustrated* magazines, lists provided by *Sports Illustrated* employees, and through snowball sampling techniques. I often experienced difficulty obtaining these interviews because these producers are very busy and/or occupy status positions with a high degree of prestige. I suspect that the controversy surrounding the swimsuit issue also led some to turn down my request for an interview.

The fifteen interviewed producers include seven women and eight men. I am aware that one of the interviewed producers is African-American and half of the these producers are European-American, while I possess no information about the race of the rest of the producers. Only one of these producers criticizes the swimsuit issue. The other interviewed producers praise the swimsuit issue and many people involved with its production.

## Recruitment of, and Information about, Interviewed Consumers

I employed a variety of sampling techniques to obtain a diverse group of consumers to interview. I started to recruit these consumers in a random fashion. I randomly selected telephone numbers out of a metropolitan telephone book that includes diverse categories of people, and then I called these numbers. I made the telephone calls in the evenings and on the weekends. Only one person who answered the telephone had not heard of the swimsuit issue. I requested an interview with the person who answered the telephone. Approximately one-quarter of the people I talked to agreed to the interview.

Although this sampling technique resulted in subjects who live in diverse areas, in urban, suburban and close-to-suburban rural areas of residence, the first fourteen interview subjects lacked diversity in regard to race, gender, and opinion regarding the swimsuit issue. These subjects were primarily white women who had a critical or neutral opinion of the swimsuit issue. So, after completing fourteen interviews, I modified my sampling technique to achieve a more diverse pool of interview subjects.

After these fourteen interviews, I used the same method to select the telephone numbers, but began to request interviews only with men in the contacted households. This practice resulted in more male interview subjects, but did not result in more people of color or individuals who enjoy the swimsuit issue.

Thus, after about twenty-six total interviews, I began to employ a purposive sampling technique. I used a variety of personal, professional, and organizational contacts to reach teenagers, people of color, known gays and lesbians, and those who enjoy the swimsuit issue.

After thirty-nine interviews, I felt satisfied with the pool of interviewed consumers in regard to their diversity of opinions and identities. I reached a point where multiple individuals in this pool articulated most of the opinions of the swimsuit issue. So, at this point, I stopped interviewing consumers.

The ages of the thirty-nine interviewed consumers range from fifteen to seventy-three. One of these consumers refused to give her age. The rest of the sample consisted of twenty-four percent teenagers, twenty-one percent people in their 20s, twenty-four percent people in their 30s, twenty-one percent people in their 40s, five percent people in their 50s, 2.5 percent people in their 60s, and 2.5 percent people in their 70s. My pursuit of consumers who enjoy the swimsuit issue during the purposive sampling phase probably caused the underrepresentation of older people in this sample.

Eighty-two percent of the interviewed consumers are white and eighteen percent are people of color: four African-Americans, one Asian-American, and two Native-Americans. Twenty interviewed consumers are men and nineteen are women.

I used five income categories to gain information about the subjects' household income. Excluding the three interviewed consumers who refused to discuss their household income, twenty-eight percent have incomes of less than $25,000, thirty-three percent have incomes of $25,000–40,000, twenty-five percent have incomes of $40,000–70,000, eleven percent have incomes of $70,000–100,000, and three percent have incomes over $100,000. Hardly any of the interviewed consumers work in the same occupation, but twenty-six percent attend school.

Most of the interviewed consumers avidly read magazines. On average, these consumers regularly read three different magazines. Collectively, these consumers read seventy-two different magazines on a regular basis. Among the more commonly read magazines, the male consumers read *Sports Illustrated* and the women read *Good Housekeeping* and *Cosmopolitan,* while *Time, Newsweek,* and *People* drew a more gender-balanced audience.

The interviewed consumers vary in regard to their sport participation. Among these consumers, the males participate in sport more than the females, but the females participate in more fitness activities.

The interviewed consumers have a variety of sport spectating habits. Although the interviewed male consumers engage in more sport spectatorship than the interviewed female consumers, many of the females engage in a considerable amount of sport spectatorship. The interviewed consumers mainly watch men's professional and college baseball, football, basketball, and ice hockey. These consumers tend to follow their "home teams." Some of them watch high school sports. Only a few of these consumers say that they watch more "minor sports," watch women's sports, or attend to coverage of social issues in sport. These consumers most commonly consume sport by attending events, watching television, and reading newspapers, rather than listening to the radio or reading magazines. Most of the interviewed consumers who read sport magazines are men.

Twenty-three percent of the interviewed consumers regularly read *Sports Illustrated,* while thirty-six percent occasionally read the magazine, and forty-one percent do not read the magazine. All of the regular readers are men, forty-three percent of the occasional readers are men, and thirty-one percent of the non-readers are men. Thirteen percent of the interviewed consumers (five consumers)—all men—subscribe to *Sports Illustrated.*

I asked the interviewed consumers if they look at the *Sports Illustrated* swimsuit issue. Twenty-eight percent regularly look at the swimsuit issue, twenty-six percent occasionally look at the issue, thirty-one percent looked at the issue once, twice, or a few times, and fifteen percent never looked at the issue. All of the interviewed consumers had heard of the swimsuit issue, and all participated in or heard some discussion about the issue. Among these consumers, ninety-one percent of the regular readers of the swimsuit issue are men, sixty percent of the occasional readers are men, seventeen percent of those who only glanced at it once or twice are men, and thirty-three percent of those who never looked at it are men. Of the sixteen interviewed male consumers who regularly and occasionally look at the swimsuit issue, five have access to the issue because they subscribe to *Sports Illustrated*, five look at a friend's issue, and two buy the issue at the newsstand. Others look at the swimsuit issue in a store, or look at the swimsuit issue that belongs to their father, brother, co-worker, or barber. Of the five interviewed female consumers who regularly and occasionally look at the swimsuit issue, four look at their husband's swimsuit issue, one looks at the issue at work, and one looks at the issue in a store. The only interviewed female consumer who regularly looks at the swimsuit issue works as a model.

Reading habits of the eleven regular consumers of the swimsuit issue vary considerably, and no patterns appear to exist. Time spent viewing the issue ranges from a ten minute glance, to looking at the issue off and on for a week, to looking at swimsuit issues retained from previous years. The absence or presence of other people while reading the issue also varies considerably, ranging from reading the issue alone, to sharing it with the rest of the family, to sharing it with friends. Sometimes consumers leave the issue in the living room where anyone else can read it, and other times they keep the issue in their bedrooms where others do not have access to it. One regular reader gives the issue to friends after he finishes with it. He states, "... you just kind of gawk and stare a little bit and flip the page, and then when it's over you put it down and give it to somebody else." A few of the interviewed consumers maintain collections of *Sports Illustrated* and thus retain the swimsuit issue each year for these collections.

# NOTES

## Chapter 1

1. In this paper, the term "feminist" refers to people who believe that men possess more power than women in society and who object to this form of inequality.

2. When I interviewed producers of the swimsuit issue, my search for encoded meanings that go beyond the basic content of the issue generally met with denial and suggestions that I was "reading way too much into" the issue. Nevertheless, most of the interviewed producers who explicitly denied that they tried to express such meanings discussed them in other parts of the conversation.

## Chapter 2

1. Despite the fact that most sports now have long seasons, and the fact that sports activities continue throughout the entire year, several of the interviewed producers insist that there are not enough sports to cover between the football and baseball seasons, and thus that one reason *Sports Illustrated* continues to publish the swimsuit issue is to fill up the magazine during this part of the year. As one of the most influential producers states, "That's the reason, the same reason [as in the early years] . . . There is a sports gap after the Superbowl, before baseball starts. It's a slow time of the year."

2. Throughout this book, when I use the term "postcolonialized" countries I put parentheses around the term "post." I use these parentheses to make two points. First, colonizers still physically occupy some of these countries. Second, although the original colonizers physically departed from most of these countries, these colonizers often retain their influence over these countries in other ways, such as through economics, politics, religion, and/or the media.

3. For the sake of readability, I sometimes cite examples in footnotes rather than in the text. In this case, examples include: December 20, 1954; June 25, 1956; January, 29, 1962.

4. For example, August 30, 1954; February 21, 1955; May 23, 1955; August 26, 1957.

5. For example, January 28, 1957; January 29, 1962; January 24, 1962.

6. For example, September 3, 1956; June 22, 1957; June 9, 1958.

*Chapter 3*

1. As Abercrombie, Hill and Turner (1984) point out, the field of semiotics has provided a useful distinction between the terms signifier, signified, and sign. As they explain, "The signifier can be a physical object, a word, or a picture of some kind. The signified is a mental concept indicated by the signifier. The sign is the association of signifier and signified" (p. 188).

2. February 9, 1981; February 10, 1986; February 9, 1987.

3. In this book, the term ideology refers to a widespread system of ideas used to make sense of and define part of the world. Ideology influences and is influenced by social actions and structures.

4. Justin Lewis (1991) contends that consumers may not interpret a media text in ways that producers prefer, but are often nevertheless encouraged by the combination of textual structure and their own cultural knowledge to create particular interpretations. Also, the ideological power of some media texts depends on their ability to appeal to different audience groups in different ways. Finally, the ability of consumers to create particular interpretations does not necessarily involve free choice, because consumers are limited by the ideological environment in which they are enmeshed.

*Chapter 4*

1. Breazeale (1994) examined the early *Esquire* magazine texts and found that these texts feature a mixture of signifiers that moderate the degree/type of sexual meaning associated with the magazine.

2. Breazeale (1994) discusses how the early *Esquire* magazine texts mixed signifiers of artistic and pornographic meaning, a mixture which influenced the degree/type of sexual meaning denoted.

*Chapter 5*

1. Scholars define ideal subject position as the type of readers that a text beckons through its structure and content, thus scholars identify the ideal subject position of a text by examining the structure and content for suggestions of the preferred identities and perspectives of potential viewers. The ideal subject position indicates the identities and perspectives of those the producers assume to prevail among the readership and/or those the producers desire to read the texts (e.g., Betterton, 1987; Morley, 1980; Mulvey, 1985). We are hailed as subjects of a particular text when we identify with the ideal subject position intimated by the text, which commonly occurs when the identities suggested by the text match our own identities. Producers fashion media texts to hail different categories of people in different ways (e.g. Fiske, 1987a; Kaplan, 1990; Williamson, 1985). The ideal subject position suggested by a particular text probably has a significant impact on the number of people from particular social categories who consume this text. Yet, as Fiske (1987b) points out, real readers are social subjects who are located in social/cultural/historical formations, and their sociocultural backgrounds greatly influence the meanings they create.

2. Breazeale (1994) argues that the early *Esquire* magazine defined its (male) readers as heterosexual through sexual representation of women.

*Chapter 6*

1. Connell (1995), whose scholarship is cited throughout this book, objects to the notion of "masculinity crisis," arguing that because masculinity is not a coherent system but "a configuration of practice *within* a system of gender relations" (p. 84) it is really the larger gender order itself that enters periods of crisis.

2. Coverage of female athletes often differs from coverage of male athletes. When the popular media cover women in sport, they often focus on the athlete's appearance (e.g., Duncan, 1990; Dickey, 1987; Hargreaves, 1986) and personal life (e.g., Dickey, 1987; Glen-Haig, 1985; Whannel, 1984). Unlike the coverage of male athletes, coverage of female athletes often portrays them as emotional (Duncan, 1990; Williams, C., Lawrence & Rowe, 1985). And, unlike the photographs of male athletes, photographs of female athletes often feature inactive glamorous poses or show the athletes in settings unrelated to athletics

(e.g., Duncan 1990; Kane, 1988; 1989; Those Who . . ., 1983). Photographers often picture male athletes in ways that signify dominance or superiority, while picturing women athletes in ways that signify submissiveness or inferiority (Duncan, 1990).

Those women's sports that many people perceive as less masculine get greater coverage than other women's sports (e.g., Boutilier & SanGiovanni, 1983; Kane, 1988; Whannel, 1984). White, young, traditionally feminine women athletes get more media attention than other women athletes (e.g., Duncan, 1990; Halpert, 1988; Hillard, 1984). And women athletes who do not conform to hegemonic feminine ideals often receive negative coverage (Clarke & Clarke, 1982; Klein, 1988).

Whereas the mass media often represent male athletes in desexualized ways (Horne, 1988; Those Who . . ., 1983), they often sexualize women athletes (e.g., Duncan, 1990; Horne, 1988; Kane, 1989). Some scholars argue that sexualization of women athletes in the mass media works to trivialize and deny power to these athletes, and thus reduces the threat these athletes represent to men's dominance in sport or to sport as a masculine preserve (Duncan & Hasbrook, 1988; Those Who . . ., 1983).

The lack of coverage of women in sport helps to reinforce the notions that sport is primarily an activity for men, and that women's sport does not deserve attention. As Felshin (1974) comments, the coverage of women's sport leads one to think ". . . that either only one or two outstanding women compete in sport at all, or that women do not compete, but when they do, it is always in a nonserious and trivial way" (p. 249). The mass media rarely addresses social conditions that influence women's sport participation and performances (Williams, C., Lawrence & Rowe, 1985).

Mass media coverage works to legitimate women's secondary position in sport and sport media coverage by highlighting perceived inherent physical differences between women and men (e.g., Duncan, 1990; Whannel, 1984; Williams, C., Lawrence & Rowe, 1985; 1986). As Duncan (1990) observes, ". . . the physical marks of femininity are highlighted and emphasized in sport pictures of women, regardless of whether the women are athletes or spectators" (p. 28). Duncan (1990) explains that, "Focusing on female differences is a political strategy that places women in a position of weakness. Sport photographs that emphasize otherness of women enable patriarchal ends" (p. 40). The media coverage displays an obvious distaste for women athletes who blur conventional gender-related physical boundaries (Klein, 1988). Media producers sometimes question the sex of these women athletes in their texts (Hargreaves, 1986).

Only a few scholars have completed research or proposed adequate theories about why sport media producers fail to equitably cover women athletes. Some suggest that media producers believe that women's sport lacks commercial value (Boutilier & SanGiovanni, 1983; Purdy, 1978). But, as Boutilier and SanGiovanni (1983) note, this is a "catch twenty-two," because women's sport will not develop a mass audience, and thus attain commercial value, without extensive media coverage. Theberge and Cronk (1986) completed the most theoretically valid study about the social forces that generate the inequitable media coverage for women athletes. They argue that men's commercialized sports and the mass media have a symbiotic relationship, and that this relationship results in less newspaper coverage of women's sports. Thus, the prejudice of media producers does not fully explain the inequity. Media production processes, including the methods of obtaining news and the definition of news itself, largely contribute to this problem. Underlying these production processes is the problematic organization of sport itself in North America (Theberge & Cronk, 1986).

As Boutilier and SanGiovanni (1983) point out, magazines are aimed more at specific segments of the general population than are newspapers and television, and thus one would expect better coverage of women's sport in some magazines. Rintala and Birrell (1984) report that although *Young Athlete* magazine draws a large proportion of girl readers and seems to contain better coverage of female athletes than most sport magazines, female athletes appear less often in photographs and more often if they participate in traditionally gender-appropriate sports. Duncan and Sayaouong (1989) studied *Sports Illustrated for Kids* magazine, and found that women appear less often in photographs, and photographs of male athletes often signify the athlete's power and dominance through the camera angle. Hollands (1984) concludes that coverage of tennis in general magazines often focuses more on male athletes, reinforces gender stereotypes, trivializes the women athletes, and highlights women athletes' gender rather than athletic prowess. So-called women's magazines rarely represent women athletes, and when these magazines do feature women athletes the primary focus of the coverage rarely involves athleticism (Boutilier & SanGiovanni, 1983). As Boutilier and SanGiovanni (1983) comment, "By employing traditional editorial themes of women's magazines—fashion, beauty, diet, dating—women's sport is getting coverage in ways that are both subtle and safe but seldom sporting" (p. 212).

Even magazines that focus specifically on women in sport do not completely avoid the problems plaguing the portrayal of women athletes (eg., Boutilier & SanGiovanni, 1983; Kane, 1989; Hillard, 1984). In the late 1970s, the magazine *Women's Sports* (previously known as *womenSports* and now titled *Women's Sports + Fitness*) began to resemble conventional women's magazines by beckoning young, affluent, white, and heterosexual women readers, pandering to gender stereotypes, and heavily covering topics such as health, fitness, beauty, nutrition, and fashion. Boutilier and SanGiovanni (1983) suggest that this shift in coverage did not stem from the interests of the readership, but from the desire for advertising dollars. The magazine faces financial difficulties, so the publishers probably altered the magazine to create a more lucrative audience for advertisers. Boutilier and SanGiovanni (1983) argue that *Women's Sports* magazine fails to challenge homophobia in sport and normative ideals of femininity.

3. Hanna (1983) argues that *Sports Illustrated* caters to mass tastes, avoiding controversy and the representation of new or critical ideas. Condor and Anderson (1984) note that for many years *Sports Illustrated* neglected to cover black athletes. Hanna (1983) contends that *Sports Illustrated* does not express a healthy skepticism of sports business and only feigns concern over social issues in sport.

4. Overall, *Sports Illustrated* is one of the most widely read magazines in the United States, ranked sixteenth overall in 1990 (*Advertising Age,* 1990). *Sports Illustrated* is the most popular weekly sports magazine in the world (e.g. Boutilier & SanGiovanni, 1983; Coakley, 1986; Erickson, 1987), with much higher figures for circulation than other sports magazines (*Advertising Age,* 1990; Erickson, 1987). A report dated June 30, 1991 (Audit Bureau of Circulation, 1991) indicates that 3,444,188 people consume each issue, 95.7 percent of whom subscribe to the magazine. One producer I interviewed claimed that five to six people read each copy of the magazine.

5. February 24, 1986, p. 77 and March 9, 1987, p. 12.

*Chapter 7*

1. For example, February 7, 1977, p. 72; February 25, 1985, p. 74; March 2, 1987, p. 7.

2. February 3, 1964, p. 62; February 19, 1979, p.78.

3. For example, articles about swimwear fashion appeared in the February 11, 1985, February 9, 1987, and February 12, 1990 swimsuit issues.

4. January 30, 1978, p. 68; February 25, 1985, p. 74; March 3, 1980, p. 74; February 25, 1985, p. 76; March 12, 1987, p. 7; February 18, 1980, p. 94; March 5, 1990, p. 4.

*Chapter 9*

1. Sabo and Snyder (1993) surveyed women who work in white-collar occupations and learned that most felt that men had more time for sport/exercise than women. Despite the fact that the married women hold jobs in the public arena, they continue to shoulder much more than half of the housework and childcare tasks. This gendered division of household labor increases the amount of time men can devote to leisure and sport/exercise and limits the amount of time women can devote to these activities.

2. The philosophy of the *Sports Illustrated* swimsuit issue parallels the philosophy of the early *Esquire* magazine and of *Playboy* magazine in this regard. The early *Esquire* magazine linked enjoyment of sexual representations of women with humor. In this way and others, *Esquire* served as a model for *Playboy* magazine (Breazeale, 1994). Interestingly, the first issue of *Playboy* was released within a year of the first issue of *Sports Illustrated*. Like *Sports Illustrated*, *Playboy* is designed to provide entertainment for affluent heterosexual men, and highlights the world of leisure and play to do so. In a manner similar to *Sports Illustrated*'s swimsuit issue, *Playboy* attempts to evoke meanings of fantasy, fun, celebration, adventure, and humor (Goldberg, 1967; Hefner, 1962-1965; Miller, 1984; Weyr, 1978). As Hefner (1962–1965) puts it, *Playboy* "is primarily concerned with the lighter side of life" (p. 13).

3. Sabo et al. (1996) studied television coverage of seven international sporting events, and found that this coverage tended to portray Asian, and perhaps Latino, athletes as exotic.

Abercrombie, N., Hill, S., & Turner, B. S. (1984). *The Penguin Dictionary of Sociology.* New York, NY: Penguin.

Adams, K. M. (1984). Come to Tana Toraja, "Land of the Heavenly Kings": Travel Agents as Brokers of Ethnicity. *Annals of Tourism, 11*(3): 469–485.

Adler J., Darnton, N. &, Barrett, T. (1989, February 13). *Newsweek:* 53–54.

*Advertising Age.* (1990, Aug. 20). Vol. *61*(24): 42.

Albers, P. C. & James, W. R. (1988). Travel Photography: A Methodological Approach. *Annals of Tourism Research, 15*(1): 134–158.

Alloula, M. (1986). *The Colonial Harem.* Minneapolis, MN: Univ. of MN.

Audit Bureau of Circulation. (1991, June 30). *Magazine Publisher's Statement: Sports Illustrated.* Schaumburg, IL.

Banner, L. (1983). *American Beauty.* New York, NY: Alfred A. Knopf.

Barthel, D. (1988). *Putting on Appearances: Gender and Advertising.* Philadelphia, PA: Temple Univ.

Bartky, S. L. (1982). Narcissism, femininity and Alienation. *Social Theory and Practice, 8*(2): 127–143.

———. (1988). Foucault, Femininity, and the Modernization of Patriarchal Power. In I. Diamond & L. Quinby (Eds.), *Feminism and Foucault: Reflections on Resistance* (pp. 61–86). Boston, MA: Northeastern Univ.

Baudrillard, J. (1981). *For a Critique of the Political Economy of the Sign.* St. Louis, MO: Telos.

Beloff, H. (1985). *Camera Culture.* New York, NY: Basil Blackwell.

Bennett, T. (1986). Introduction: Popular Culture and 'the Turn to Gramsci'. In T. Bennett, C. Mercer & J. Woollacott (Eds.), *Popular Culture and Social Relations* (pp. xi–xix). Philadelphia, PA: Open Univ.

Berger, A. A. (1982). *Media Analysis Techniques.* Beverley Hills, CA: Sage.

Berger, J. (1985). *Ways of Seeing.* London, England: British Broadcasting Network and Penguin.

Betterton, R. (1985). How do Women Look? The Female Nude in the Work of Suzanne Valedon. *Feminist Review, 19:* 3–24.

———. (1987). *Looking On: Images of Femininity in the Visual Arts and Media.* New York, NY: Pandora.

Boutilier, M. A. & SanGiovanni, L. (1983). *The Sporting Woman.* Champaign, IL: Human Kinetics.

Breazeale, K. (1994). In Spite of Women: *Esquire* Magazine and the Construction of the Male Consumer. *Signs: A Journal of Women in Culture and Society, 20*(1): 1–22.

Brod, H. (1984). Ethos Thanatized: Pornography and Male Sexuality. *Humanities in Society, 7*(1/2): 47–63.

Buchbinder, H. (1987). Male Heterosexuality: The Socialized Penis Revisited. In H. Buchbinder, V. Burstyn, D. Forbes & M. Steedman (Eds.), *Who's on Top? The Politics of Heterosexuality* (pp. 63–82). Toronto, Ontario, Canada: Garamond.

Budd, M., Entman, R. M. & Steinman, C. (1990). The Affirmative Character of U.S. Cultural Studies. *Critical Studies in Mass Communication, 7:* 169–184.

Bulbeck, C. (1988). *One World Women's Movement.* London, England: Pluto.

Canadian Association for the Advancement of Women and Sports and Physical Activity. (1990s). *Words to Watch* and *Women in Motion: Guidelines for Non-Sexist Language and Visual Materials.* Gloucester, Ontario, Canada: Canadian Association for the Advancement of Women and Sport and Physical Activity.

Caputi, J. (1983). One Size Does Not Fit All: Being Beautiful, Thin and Female in America. In C. D. Geist & J. Nachbar (Eds.), *The Popular Culture Reader* (3rd Ed.) (pp. 186–204). Bowling Green, OH: Bowling Green Univ. Popular Press.

Carby, H. V. (1982). White Woman Listen! Black Feminism and the Boundaries of Sisterhood. In Centre for Contemporary Cultural Studies (Eds.), *The Empire Strikes Back: Race and Racism in 70s Britain* (pp. 212–235). London, England: Hutchinson & Co.

Carrigan, T., Connell, B. & Lee, J. (1987). Toward a New Sociology of Masculinity. In H. Brod (Ed.), *The Making of Masculinities* (pp. 63–100). Boston, MA: Allen & Unwin.

Chapkis, W. (1986). *Beauty Secrets: Women and the Politics of Appearance.* Boston, MA: South End.

Chorbajian, L. (1978). The Social Psychology of American Males and Spectator Sports. *International Review for Sociology of Sport 9:* 165–175.

Chroni, S., Bunker, L. K. & Sabo, D. (1995). *Out of the Picture: Gender Bias and Children's Perceptions of the Proposed Pictograms for the 1996 Olympic Games.* East Meadow, NY: Women's Sports Foundation.

Clarke, A. & Clarke, J. (1982). 'Highlights and Action Replays'—Ideology, Sport and the Media. In J. Hargreaves (Ed.), *Sport, Culture and Ideology* (pp. 62–87). London, England: Routledge & Kegan Paul.

Clifford, J. (1987). In H. Foster (Ed.), *Discussions in Contemporary Culture* (pp. 121–130). Seattle, WA: Bay.

Coakley, J. J. (1986). *Sport in Society: Issues and Controversies* (3rd Ed.). St. Louis, MO: Times Mirror/Mosby.

Condit, C. M. (1989). The Rhetorical Limits of Polysemy. *Critical Studies in Mass Communication, 6*(2): 103–122.

Condor, R. & Anderson, D. F. (1984). Longitudinal Analysis of Coverage Accorded Black and White Athletes in Feature Articles of *Sports Illustrated* (1960–1980). *Journal of Sport Behavior, 7*(1): 39–43.

Connell, R. W. (1987). *Gender and Power: Society, the Person and Sexual Politics.* Stanford, CA: Stanford Univ.

————. (1990). An Iron Man: The Body and Some Contradictions of Hegemonic Masculinity. In M. A. Messner & D. F. Sabo (Eds.), *Sport, Men and the Gender Order: Critical Feminist Perspectives* (pp. 83–95). Champaign, IL: Human Kinetics.

————. (1995). *Masculinities.* Berkeley, CA: University of California Press.

Corbey, R. (1988). Alterity: The Colonial Nude. *Critique of Anthropology, 8*(3): 75–92.

Courtney, A. E. & Whipple, T. W. (1983). *Sex Stereotyping in Advertising.* Lexington, MA: Lexington Books.

Coward, R. (1985). *Female Desires: How They are Sought, Bought and Packaged.* New York, NY: Grove.

Curran, J., Gurevitch, M. & Woollacott, J. (1982). The Study of the Media: Theoretical Approaches. In M. Gurevitch, T. Bennett, J. Curran & J. Woollacott (Eds.), *Culture, Society and the Media* (pp. 11–29). New York, NY: Methuen.

Davis, A. Y. (1983). *Women, Race and Class.* New York, NY: Vintage.

Davis, L. R. (1993). Critical Analysis of the Popular Media and the Concept of Ideal Subject Position: *Sports Illustrated* as Case Study. *Quest, 45*(2): 165–181.

————. (1994). A Postmodern Paradox? Cheerleaders at Women's Sporting Events. In S. Birrell & C. L. Cole (Eds.), *Women, Sport, and Culture* (pp. 149–158). Campaign, IL: Human Kinetics

Deford, F. (1989). How It All Began. *Sports Illustrated, 70*(6): 38–47.

DeMont, J. (1989, February 20). Tapping a Market: Swimsuit Magazines are Earning Bit Profits. *Macleans, 102*(8): 28.

Desnoes, E. (1985). Cuba Made Me So. In M. Blonsky (Ed.), *On Signs* (pp. 384–403). Baltimore, MD: John Hopkins Univ.

———. (1988). The Photographic Image of Underdevelopment. *Jump Cut, 33:* 69–81.

Dickey, J. (1987). Heterosexism and the Lesbian Image in the Press. In K. Davies, J. Dickey & T. Stratford (Eds.), *Out of Focus: Writings on Women and the Media* (pp. 81–89). London, England: The Women's Press.

Doane, M. A. (1987). *The Desire to Desire: The Women's Film of the 1940s.* Bloomington, IN: Indiana Univ.

Don Bowden Associates. (1988, April). *The Subscribing Households of* Sports Illustrated: *National Edition.* New York, NY: Time, Inc.

Dorfman, A. & Mattelart, A. (1975). *How to Read Donald Duck: Imperialist Ideology in the Disney Comic.* New York, NY: International General.

Dubbert, J. L. (1979). *A Man's Place: Masculinity in Transition.* Englewood Cliffs, NJ: Prentice-Hall.

Duncan, M. C. (1990). Sport Photographs and Sexual Difference: Images of Women and Men in the 1984 and 1988 Olympic Games. *Sociology of Sport Journal, 7:* 22–43.

———. (1993). Beyond Analyses of Sport Media Texts: An Argument for Formal Analysis of Institutional Structures. *Sociology of Sport Journal, 10*(4): 353–372.

Duncan, M. C. & Hasbrook, C. A. (1988). Denial of Power in Televised Women's Sports. *Sociology of Sport Journal, 5*(1): 1–21.

Duncan, M. C. & Messner, M. A. (1991, January). *Coverage of Women's Sports in Four Daily Newspapers.* Los Angeles, CA: Amateur Athletic Foundation of Los Angeles.

Duncan, M. C., Messner, M. A., Jensen, K. & Wachs, F. L. (1994, July). *Gender Stereotyping in Televised Sports: A Follow-Up to the 1989 Study.* Los Angeles, CA: Amateur Athletic Foundation of Los Angeles.

Duncan, M. C., Messner, M. A., Williams, L. & Jensen, K. (1990, August). *Gender Stereotyping in Televised Sports.* Los Angeles, CA: Amateur Athletic Foundation of Los Angeles.

Duncan, M. C. & Sayaouong, A. (1989). Visual Images and Gender in *Sports Illustrated for Kids.* Presented at N.A.S.S.S. meeting, November 8–12, Washington, DC.

Duquin, M. E. (1989). Fashion and Fitness: Images in Women's Magazine Advertisements. *Arena Review, 13*(2): 97–109.

Dyer, G. (1987). Women and Television: An Overview. In H. Baehr & G. Dyer (Eds.). *Boxed In: Women and Television* (pp. 6–16). New York, NY: Pandora.

Dyer, R. (1982). Don't Look Now. *Screen, 23*(3/4): 61–73.

———. (1985). Male Sexuality in the Media. In A. Metcalf & M. Humphries (Eds.), *The Sexuality of Men* (pp. 28–43). London, England: Pluto.

Eitzen, D. S. & Sage, G. H. (1982). *Sociology of American Sport* (2nd Ed.). Dubuque, IA: Wm. C. Brown.

Elliott, S. (1989, February 6). The Magazine is a Market of Its Own. *USA Today:* D4.

Elliott, S. (1994, February 16). Advertising: Holy Pecs! *Sports Illustrated's* 1994 Swimsuit Issue Includes Pictures of Some Topless Models. *The New York Times:* C2.

Ellsworth, E. (1984). Incorporation of Feminist Meanings in Media Texts. *Humanities in Society, 7*(1/2): 65–75.

Enloe, C. (1983). *Does Khaki Become You?* Boston, MA: South End.

Erickson, J. L. (1987, July 13). Foes Try Hard, but *'SI'* Still Laps the Field. *Advertising Age, 58:* 5–20.

Fasteau, M. F. (1980). Sports: The Training Ground. In D. F. Sabo & R. Runfola (Eds.), *Jock: Sports & Male Identity* (pp. 44–53). Englewood Cliffs, NJ: Prentice-Hall.

Felshin, J. (1974). Social Commentary. In E. W. Gerber, J. Felshin, P. Berlin & W. Wyrick (Eds.), *The American Women in Sport* (pp. 249–279). Reading, MA: Addison-Wesley.

Ferguson, M. (1983). *Forever Feminine: Women's Magazines and the Cult of Femininity.* London, England: Heinemann Educational Books.

Ferran, D. (1987). A Photography of Marilyn Monroe. *Studies in Sexual Politics, 16:* 22.

Fine, S. A. (1987). *With the Boys.* Chicago, IL: Univ. of Chicago.

Finn, G. (1985). Patriarchy and Pleasure: The Pornographic Eye/I. *Canadian Journal of Political and Social Theory, 9*(1/2): 81–95.

Fishburn, K. (1982). *Women in Popular Culture: A Reference Guide.* Westport, CT: Greenwood.

Fiske, J. (1987a). British Cultural Studies and Television. In R. C. Allen (Ed.), *Channels of Discourse: Television and Contemporary Criticism* (pp. 254–289). Chapel Hill, NC: Univ. of NC.

———. (1987b). *Television Culture.* New York, NY: Methuen & Co.

Ford, A. (1982). The Sports Novel as a Popular Genre. In Dept. of Physical Education and the Centre for Contemporary Cultural Studies (Eds.), *Sporting Fictions* (pp. 232–248). Birmingham, England: Univ. of Birmingham.

Freedman, R. J. (1986). *Beauty Bound.* Lexington, MA: Lexington Books.

Freund, G. (1980). *Photography and Society.* Boston, MA: David R.Godine.

Gabor, M. (1973). *The Pin-up: A Modest History.* New York, NY: Universe.

Gagnon, J. H. (1976). Physical Strength, Once of Significance. In D. S. David & R. Brannon (Eds.), *The Forty-Nine Percent Majority: The Male Sex Role* (pp. 169–178). Reading, MA: Addison-Wesley.

Gardner, T. A. (1980). Racism in Pornography and the Women's Movement. In L. Lederer (Ed.), *Take Back the Night* (pp. 105–114). New York, NY: William Morrow.

Glen-Haig, M. A. (1985). The Applause of Women as Recompense. *Message Olympique, 12:* 9–18.

Goffman, E. (1976). *Gender Advertisements.* New York, NY: Harper Colophon.

Goldberg, J. (1967). *Big Bunny: The Inside Story of 'Playboy'.* New York, NY: Ballantine.

Graburn, N. H. H. (1984). The Evolution of Tourist Arts. *Annals of Tourism Research, 11*(1): 393–419.

Graham, D. (1987). Discussion. In H. Foster (Ed.), *Discussions in Contemporary Culture* (pp. 105–118). Seattle, WA: Bay Press.

Graham-Brown, S. (1988). *Images of Women: The Portrayal of Women in Photography of the Middle East 1860–1950.* New York, NY: Columbia Univ.

Green, M. & Jenkins, C. (1982). Introduction. In Dept. of Physical Education and the Centre for Contemporary Cultural Studies (Eds.), *Sporting Fictions* (pp. 1–6). Birmingham, England: Univ. of Birmingham.

Greendorfer, S. L. (1983). Sport and the Mass Media: General Overview. *Arena Review, 7*(2): 1–6.

Gupta, S. (1986). Northern Media, Southern Lives. In P. Holland, J. Spence & S.Whatney (Eds.), *Photography/Politics: Two* (pp. 162–166). London, England: Comedia.

Hall, S. (1977). Culture, the Media and the 'Ideological Effect'. In J. Curran, M. Gurevitch & J. Woollacott (Eds.). *Mass Communication and Society* (pp. 315–348). London, England: Open Univ.

———. (1984). Encoding/Decoding. In S. Hall, D. Hobson, A. Lowe & P. Willis (Eds.), *Culture, Media, Language: Working Papers in Cultural Studies, 1972–79* (pp. 128–138). London, England: Hutchinson & The Centre for Contemporary Cultural Studies, Univ. of Birmingham.

Halpert, F. E. (1988). You Call This Adorable? An Open Letter to the Producer of NBC Sports. *Ms., 17*(4): 36–39.

Hanna, J. (1983). Some Comments on Sports Commentators. In W. J. Baker & J. A. Rog (Eds.), *Sports and the Humanities: A Symposium* (pp. 69–84). Orono, ME: Univ. of ME at Orono.

Haraway, D. (1984/1985). Teddy Bear Patriarchy: Taxidermy in the Garden of Eden, New York City, 1908–1936. *Social Text, 4*(2): 20–64.

———. (1989). Monkeys, Aliens, and Women: Love, Science and the Politics at the Intersection of Feminist Theory and Colonial Discourse. *Women's Studies International Forum, 12*(3): 295–312.

Hargreaves, J. A. (1986). Where's the Virtue? Where's the Grace? A Discussion of the Social Production of Gender Relations in and through Sport. *Theory, Culture and Society, 3:* 79–90.

Hart, A. (1989). Images of the Third World. *Links, 34:* 12–17.

Hearn, J. (1985). Men's Sexuality at Work. In A. Metcalf & M. Humphries (Eds.), *The Sexuality of Men* (pp. 110–128). London, England: Pluto.

Heck, M. C. (1984). The Ideological Dimension of Media Messages. In S. Hall, D. Hobson, A. Lowe & P. Willis (Eds.), *Culture, Media, Language* (pp. 122–127). London, England: Hutchinson & The Centre for Contemporary Cultural Studies.

Hefner, H. (1962–1965). *The 'Playboy' Philosophy.* Chicago, IL: HMH/Playboy.

Herek, G. M. (1986). On Heterosexual Masculinity. *American Behavior Scientist, 29*(5): 563–577.

Hillard, D. C. (1984). Media Images of Male and Female Professional Athletes: An Interpretive Analysis of Magazine Articles. *Sociology of Sport Journal, 1:* 251–262.

Hite, S. (1981). *The Hite Report on Male Sexuality.* New York, NY: Alfred A. Knopf.

Hoch, P. (1979). *White Hero, Black Beast: Racism, Sexism and the Mask of Masculinity.* London, England: Pluto Press.

Hollands, R. G. (1984). Images of Women in Canadian Sport Fiction. In N. Theberge & P. Donnelly (Eds.), *Sport and the Sociological Imagination* (pp. 40–56). Fort Worth, TX: Texas Christian Univ.

hooks, b. (1988). Straightening Our Hair. *Zeta Magazine, 1*(9): 33–37.

Horne, J. (1988). *Generalist Sports Magazines in the USA and UK: Researching Representations of Sport.* Presented at N.A.S.S.S. meeting, November 9–12, Cincinnati, OH.

Horowitz, G. & Kaufman, M. (1987). Male Sexuality: Toward a Theory of Liberation. In M. Kaufman (Ed.), *Beyond Patriarchy: Essays by Men on Pleasure, Power, and Change* (pp. 81–102). New York, NY: Oxford Univ.

Howell, M. (1988). Finding the Real Me. *Minnesota Women's Press, 3*(23): 1–2.

Jan Mohamed, A. R. & Llyod, D. (1987). Introduction: Minority Discourse—What is to be done? *Cultural Critique, 7:* 5–18.

Joseph, G. I. (1981). The Media and Blacks—Selling It Like It Isn't. In G. L. Joseph & J. Lewis, *Common Differences: Conflicts in Black and White Feminist Perspectives* (pp. 151–165). Garden City, NY: Anchor.

Kane, M. J. (1988). Media Coverage of the Female Athlete Before, During and After Title IX: *Sports Illustrated* Revisited. *Journal of Sport Management, 2:* 87–89.

———. (1989). The Post Title IX Female Athlete in the Media: Things are Changing, But How Much? *J.O.P.E.R.D., 60*(3): 58–62.

Kang, J. (1988). Sports, Media and Cultural Dependency. *Journal of Contemporary Asia, 18*(4): 430–443.

Kaplan, E. A. (1990). In J. Bergstrom & M. A. Doane (Eds.), The Spectatrix, *Camera Obscura, 20/21:* 194–199.

Kappeler, S. (1986). *The Pornography of Representation.* Minneapolis, MN: Univ. of MN.

Kimmel, M. S. (1990). Baseball and the Reconstitution of American Masculinity, 1880–1920. In M. A. Messner & D. F. Sabo (Eds.), *Sport, Men and the Gender Order: Critical Feminist Perspectives* (pp. 55–66). Champaign, IL: Human Kinetics.

Kinsman, G. (1987). *The Regulation of Desire: Sexuality in Canada.* New York, NY: Black Rose.

Klein, M. (1988). Women in the Discourse of Sport Reports. *International Review for Sociology of Sport, 23*(2): 139–152.

Kuhn, A. (1985). *The Power of the Image: Essays on Representation and Sexuality.* Boston, MA: Routledge & Kegan Paul.

Lakoff, R. T. & Scherr, R. L. (1984). *Face Value: The Politics of Beauty.* Boston, MA: Routledge & Kegan Paul.

Leiss. W., Kline, S. & Jhally, S. (1986). *Social Communication in Advertising.* New York, NY: Methuen.

Lewallen, A. (1988). *Lace:* Pornography for Women? In L. Gamman & M. Marshment (Eds.), *The Female Gaze: Women as Viewers of Popular Culture* (pp. 86–101). London, England: The Women's Press.

Lewis, J. (1991). *The Ideological Octopus: An Exploration of Television and Its Audience.* New York, NY: Routledge.

Lieberman, D. (1989, January 16). *SI*'s Swimsuit Issue: More than Meets the Eye. *Business Week, 3087:* 52.

Litewka, J. (1977). The Socialized Penis. In J. Snodgrass (Ed.), *For Men Against Sexism* (pp. 16–35). Albion, CA: Times Change.

Lumpkin, A. & Williams, L. (1989). *An Analysis of the Sport, Gender, Race, Sporting Role, and Descriptive Characteristics of All Individuals Featured in* Sports Illustrated, *1954–1987*. Presented at A.A.H.P.E.R.D. meeting.

Lurie, A. (1981). *The Language of Clothes*. New York, NY: Random House.

MacCannel, D. (1976). *The Tourist: A New Theory of the Leisure Class*. New York, NY: Schocken.

———. (1984). Reconstructed Ethnicity: Tourism and Cultural Identity in Third World Communities. *Annals of Tourism Research, 11*(3): 375–391.

Manning, F. E. (1977). Cup Match and Carnival: Secular Rites of Revitalization in Decolonizing, Tourist-Oriented Societies. In S. F. Moore & B. G. Myerhoff (Eds.), *Secular Ritual* (pp. 265–281). Assen/Amsterdam, Netherlands: Van Gorcum.

Masse, M. A. & Rosenblum, K. (1988). Male and Female Created They Them: The Depiction of Gender in Advertising of Traditional Women's and Men's Magazines. *Women's Studies International Forum, 11*(2): 127–144.

McKay, J. & Rowe, D. (1987). Ideology, the Media, and Australian Sport. *Sociology of Sport Journal, 4:* 258–273.

Messner, M. (1987). The Meaning of Success: The Athletic Experience and the Development of Male Identity. In H. Brod (Ed.), *The Making of Masculinities* (pp. 193–209). Boston, MA: Allen & Unwin.

———. (1988). *When Bodies are Weapons: Masculinity and Violence in Sport*. Paper presented at N.A.S.S.S. meeting, November, Cincinnati, OH.

———. (1992). *Power at Play: Sport and the Problem of Masculinity*. Boston, MA: Beacon Press.

Metcalf, A. (1985). Introduction. In A. Metcalf & M. Humphries (Eds.), *The Sexuality of Men* (pp. 1–14). London, England: Pluto Press.

Meyers, K. (1982a). Fashion 'N' Passion. *Screen, 23*(3/4): 89–97.

———. (1982b). Toward a Feminist Erotica. *Camerawork, 24:* 14–19.

Meyrowitz, J. (1985). *No Sense of Place: The Impact of the Electronic Media on Social Behavior*. New York, NY: Oxford Univ.

Miller, R. (1984). *Bunny: The Real Story of 'Playboy'*. New York, NY: Holt, Rinehart & Winston.

Millum, T. (1975). *Images of Woman: Advertising in Women's Magazines*. Totowa, NJ: Rowman and Littlefield.

Mishkind, M. E., Rodin, J., Silberstein, L. R. & Striegel-Moore, R. H. (1986). The Embodiment of Masculinity. *American Behavior Scientist, 29*(5): 545–562.

Morley, D. (1980). *The 'Nationwide' Audience: Structure and Decoding.* London, England: British Film Institute.

Morse, M. (1983). Sport on Television: Replay and Display. In E. A. Kaplan (Ed.), *Regarding Television: Critical Approaches—An Anthology* (pp. 44–66). Bethesda, MD: University Publications of America.

Mulvey, L. (1985). Visual Pleasure and Narrative Cinema. In G. Mast & M. Cohen (Eds.), *Film Theory and Criticism* (3rd Ed.) (pp. 803–816). New York, NY: Oxford Univ.

———. (1988). Afterthoughts on 'Visual Pleasure and Narrative Cinema' Inspired by *Duel in the Sun.* In C. Penley (Ed.), *Feminism and Film Theory* (pp. 69–79). New York, NY: Routledge.

Murdock, G. (1982). Large Corporations and the Control of the Communications Industries. In M. Gurevitch, T. Bennett, J. Curran & J. Woollacott (Eds.), *Culture, Society and the Media* (pp. 118–150). New York, NY: Methuen.

Nash, R. (1979). The Exporting and Importing of Nature: Nature-Appreciation as a Commodity 1850–1980. *Perspectives in American History, 12:* 519–560.

Newman, B. (1989). Up Against the Wall. *Sports Illustrated, 70*(6): 222–228.

Okazawa-Rey, M., Robinson, T. & Ward, J. V. (1987). Black Women and the Politics of Skin Color and Hair. *Women & Therapy, 6*(1/2): 89–101.

Omolade, B. (1983). Hearts of Darkness. In A. Snitow, C. Stansell & S. Thompson (Eds.), *Powers of Desire: The Politics of Sexuality* (pp. 350–367). New York, NY: Monthly Review.

O'Sullivan, T., Hartley, J., Saunders, J., Montgomery, M. & Fiske, J. (1994). *Key Concepts in Communication and Cultural Studies.* New York, NY: Routledge.

Peiss, K. (1989). Passion and Power: An Introduction. In K. Peiss & C. Simons (Eds.), *Passion and Power: Sexuality in History* (pp. 3–13). Philadelphia, PA: Temple Univ.

Peterson, T. (1964). *Magazines in the Twentieth Century.* Urbana, IL: Univ. of IL.

Poe, A. (1976). Active Women in Ads. *Journal of Communication, 26*(4): 185–192.

Pronger, B. (1990). *The Arena of Masculinity: Sports, Homosexuality, and the Meaning of Sex.* New York, NY: St. Martin's Press.

Purdy, K. (1978). Fair Coverage. *Branching Out, 5*(4): 6–9.

Reid, L. N. & Soley, L. C. (1979). *Sports Illustrated's* Coverage of Women in Sports. *Journalism Quarterly, 56*(4): 861–863.

Renson, R. & Careel, C. (1986). Sporticuous Consumption: An Analysis of Social Status Symbolism in Sport Ads. *International Review for Sociology of Sport, 21*(2/3): 153–171.

Reynaud, E. (1983). *Holy Virility: The Social Construction of Masculinity.* London, England: Pluto.

Rintala, J. & Birrell, S. (1984). Fair Treatment for the Active Female: A Content Analysis of *Young Athlete* Magazine. *Sociology of Sport Journal, 1:* 231–250.

Robinson L. (1985). Media Invisibles. *The Crisis, 92*(6): 36–39.

Root, J. (1984). *Pictures of Women: Sexuality.* Boston, MA: Pandora.

Rosenblum, B. (1978). *Photographers at Work.* New York, NY: Holmes & Meier.

Sabo, D., Jansen, S. C., Tate, D., Duncan, M. C. & Leggett, S. (1996). Televising International Sport: Race, Ethnicity, and Nationalistic Bias. *Journal of Sport and Social Issues, 20*(1): 7–21.

Sabo, D. & Snyder, M. (1993). *Miller Lite Report on Sports & Fitness in the Lives of Working Women.* East Meadow, NY: Women's Sports Foundation, Working Women Magazine, and Miller Brewing Company.

Said, E. W. (1978). *Orientalism.* New York, NY: Pantheon.

Scott, R. (1989). The Dark Continent: Africa as Female Body in Haggard's Adventure Fiction. *Feminist Review, 32:* 69–89.

Sheard, K. & Dunning, E. (1973). The Rugby Football Club as a Type of Male Preserve. Some Sociological Notes. *International Review of Sport Sociology, 5*(3): 5–24.

Simmons Market Research Bureau. (1991, July). *1991 SMRB Study Prepared by* Sports Illustrated, *4-Color Page Rates.*

Smith, D. E. (1988). Femininity as Discourse. In L. G. Roman & L. K. Christian-Smith (Eds.), *Becoming Feminine: The Politics of Popular Culture* (pp. 37–59). Philadelphia, PA: Falmer.

Smith, L. W. (1996, February 29). *Personal correspondence.* Chapel Hill, NC: Linnea Smith.

Sontag, S. (1978). *On Photography.* New York, NY: Farrar, Straus and Giroux.

Stedman, N. (1989, March 19). Mixed Motives. *St. Paul Pioneer Press Dispatch:* 1E.

Steinem, G. (1990). Sex, Lies & Advertising. *Ms.: The World of Women, 1*(1): 18–28.

Theberge, N. & Cronk, A. (1986). Work Routines in Newspaper Sport Departments and the Coverage of Women's Sports. *Sociology of Sports Journal, 3*(3): 195–203.

Thitsa, K. (1981). Providence and Prostitution. *Spare Rib, 103:* 5–8.

Thomas, A. & Bernstein, H. (1985). *The "Third World" and "Development"*. Milton Keyes, England: Open Univ.

Those Who Own Mass Media are Teaching Millions to View Girls and Women in Sports as Sex Objects. (1983). *Media Report to Women, 11*(4): 11–12.

Time, Inc. (1993a). *Sports Illustrated* [Advertising] Rate Card #51. Effective January 10, 1994.

――――. (1993b). *Sports Illustrated* [Advertising] Rate Card for the 1994 Swimsuit Issue.

Trujillo, N. (1991). Hegemonic Masculinity on the Mound: Media Representations of Nolan Ryan and American Sports Culture. *Critical Studies in Mass Communication, 8*(3): 290–308.

Turow, J. (1984). Pressure Groups and Television Entertainment: A Framework for Analysis. In W. D. Rowland & B. Watkins (Eds.), *Interpreting Television: Current Research Perspectives* (pp. 142–162). Beverley Hills, CA: Sage.

Urry, J. (1990). *The Tourist Gaze: Leisure and Travel in Contemporary Societies*. Newbury Park, CA: Sage.

Van den Berghe, P. L. & Keyes, C. F. (1984). Introduction: Tourism and Re-Created Ethnicity. *Annals of Tourism Research, 11*(3): 343–352.

Walkerdine, V. (1984). Some Day My Prince Will Come: Young Girls and Preparation for Adolescent Sexuality. In A. McRobbie & M. Nava (Eds.), *Gender and Generation* (pp. 162–184). Hundsmills, England: McMillan.

Weir, L. & Casey, L. (1984). Subverting Power in Sexuality. *Socialist Review, 75/76:* 139–157.

Weyr, T. (1978). *Reaching for Paradise: The 'Playboy' Version of America*. New York, NY: Times.

Whannel, G. (1984). Fields of Vision: Sport and Representation. *Screen, 25*(13): 99–107.

――――. (1985). Television Spectacle and the Internationalization of Sport. *Journal of Communication, 9*(2): 54–94.

Williams, C. L., Lawrence, G. & Rowe, D. (1985). Women and Sport: A Lost Ideal. *Women's Studies International Forum, 8*(6): 639–645.

Williams, C. L., Lawrence, G. & Rowe, D. (1986). Patriarchy, Media and Sport. In G. Lawrence & D. Rowe (Eds.), *Power Play: Essays in the Sociology of Australian Sport* (pp. 215–229). Sidney, Australia: Hale & Iremonger.

Williams, L. & Lumpkin, A. (1989). *An Examination of Sport, Race, Gender, and Role of the Individuals Appearing on the Covers of* Sports Illustrated, *1954–1987*. Unpublished paper.

Williamson, J. (1985). *Decoding Advertisements.* New York, NY: Marion Boyars.

———. (1986). Woman is an Island: Femininity and Colonization. In T. Modleski (Ed.), *Studies in Entertainment: Critical Approaches to Mass Culture* (pp. 99–118). Bloomington, IN: Univ. of IN.

Willis, P. (1982). Women in Sport and Ideology. In J. A. Hargreaves (Ed.), *Sport, Culture and Ideology* (pp. 117–135). London, England: Routledge & Kegan Paul.

Wilson, C. C. & Gutierrez, F. (1985). *Minorities and Media.* Beverley Hills, CA: Sage.

Wilson, W. (1996, February 14). *Telephone Interview with Vice-President of Research at Zaffron Library of Amateur Athletic Foundation of Los Angeles.*

Winship, J. (1984). Sexuality for Sale. In S. Hall, D. Hobson, A. Lowe & P. Willis (Eds.), *Culture, Media, Language: Working Papers in Cultural Studies, 1972–79* (pp. 217–223). London, England: Hutchinson & The Centre for Contemporary Cultural Studies, Univ. of Birmingham.

———. (1987). *Inside Women's Magazines.* New York, NY: Pandora.

Women's Sports Foundation. (1995). *Images and Words in Women's Sports.* East Meadow, NY: Women's Sports Foundation.

Wood, R. E. (1984). Ethnic Tourism, the State, and Cultural Change in Southeast Asia. *Annals of Tourism Research, 11*(3): 353–374.

Woodhouse, A. (1989). *Fantastic Women: Sex, Gender and Transvestism.* New Brunswick, NJ: Rutgers Univ.

Woollacott, J. (1982). Messages and Meanings. In M. Gurevitch, T. Bennett, J. Curran & J. Woollacott (Eds.), *Culture, Society and the Media* (pp. 91–111). New York, NY: Methuen.

Wren-Lewis, J. (1983). The Encoding/Decoding Model: Criticisms and Redevelopments for Research on Decoding. *Media, Culture and Society, 5:* 179–197.

# INDEX

## A

ableism, 26

activism, directed at media (*see* media, activism)

advertising

    desire for particular audience, 58, 120

    desire for sport audience (*see* sports coverage, as desirable to advertisers)

    genre of, 39

    influence on media, 58, 120, 144n

    and profit for media, 58, 120, 144n

    rates for *Sports Illustrated* and the swimsuit issue (*see* profitability, of *Sports Illustrated*, and advertising)

    and *Sports Illustrated*, 62

    and the swimsuit issue, 16, 39

    swimsuit issue as, 61–63, 66

    critique of, 33, 66

ageism, 26

art, 38–39, 140n

audience (media). *See* consumers, influence on meanings

audience of *Sports Illustrated. See* consumers of *Sports Illustrated*

audience of the swimsuit issue. *See* consumers of the swimsuit issue

## B

bathing suits. *See* fashion, swimwear

beauty

    as meaning of the swimsuit issue, 13, 19, 22, 25–26, 30

    and racism (*see* racism, and the beauty ideal)

    and sexism (*see* sexism, and the beauty ideal)

    signifiers of, 13, 25–27, 30

    social construction of the ideal, 19, 26, 82, 89

    and *Sports Illustrated*, in the early years of the magazine, 13–14

## C

censorship of the swimsuit issue. *See* sexual representation, and the swimsuit issue, objection to

circulation rates of *Sports Illustrated. See* popularity, of *Sports Illustrated*

circulation rates of the swimsuit issue. *See* popularity, of the swimsuit issue

colonialism, 97, 107, 110, 111, 112, 113, 114, 115. *See also* symbolic colonialism